The Skin I'm In

Racism, Sports and Education

Christopher M. Spence

Fernwood Publishing

To Briana, Chandra and Taylor
and to my parents Sydney and Enez, who are celebrating
their 40th anniversary this year—congratulations!

Editing: Douglas Beall
Front cover photos: Zelia Tavares
                    University of Utah Sports Marketing Department
Back cover photo: Robert Reid
Design and production: Beverley Rach
Printed and bound in Canada by: Hignell Printing Limited

A publication of:
Fernwood Publishing
Box 9409, Station A
Halifax, Nova Scotia
B3K 5S3

Fernwood Publishing Company Limited gratefully acknowledges the financial
support of the Ministry of Canadian Heritage and the Canada Council for the
Arts for our publishing program.

Le Conseil des Arts | The Canada Council
du Canada | for the Arts

Canadian Cataloguing in Publication Data

Spence, Christopher Michael, 1962–

The skin I'm in

Includes bibliographical references.
ISBN 1-55266-017-6

1. Afro-American athletes.   2. Athletes, Black - Canada.   3. Afro-
American students -- Education.   4. Students, Black --
Education -- Canada.   5. Discrimination in sports -- North America.
6. Discrimination in education -- North America.   I. Title

GV706.32.S63 1999   796.'089'96073   C99-950197-6

Contents

Acknowledgements

I would first like to thank my parents, Sydney and Enez Spence. Your support and sacrifices have made this accomplishment our reality. I want to thank my brother Everard and sister Jacqueline for their belief in me, and my wife Marcia, who has been a reservoir of support.

Dr. George Dei continues to inspire me with his vision to uplift our race, and his encouragement, guidance and mentorship have been essential to the completion of this book. Your high expectations challenged me every step of the way. Thank you.

Dr. Helen Lenskyj willingly shared her time, knowledge and resources. Your commitment to excellence and your comments and suggestions were crucial to the development of my research.

Dr. Ted Harvey has shown me patience, empathy and support throughout my graduate pursuits. You have contributed freely of your time and experience and I am indeed grateful.

I want to thank Dr. Jim Ryan and Dr. Susan Padro for their fairness and compassion, and for being professionals of the highest standard.

I owe a debt of gratitude to Dr. Carl James for his support and willingness to share his knowledge and for his valued suggestions in the area of sport sociology.

I would like to thank the teachers, students and administrators who took time out of their schedules to share their insights. And I am also grateful to my colleagues and friends at Oakdale Park Middle School, Brookview Middle School, Lawrence Heights Middle School, Bathurst Heights High School and Westview High School, for their support, encouragement and ideas. The faculty of the Sociology Department at the Ontario Institute for Studies in Education has provided me with the opportunity for a relevant learning experience, and I wish to thank them as well as York University for giving me the opportunity to share my ideas. And my friends and family in Windsor, Kitchener, Calgary and Vancouver for their generousity and love.

Finally, I thank Errol Sharpe and Fernwood Publishing for your commitment, interest and support in bringing this much-needed project to fruition. Thank you to all those who worked on the production of the book: Douglas Beall for editing; Chauna James for typing and Beverley Rach for design and layout.

I hope to make you all proud.

Tribute

A people without knowledge of their history is like a tree without roots. —Marcus Garvey

I would be remiss to begin this book without paying my respects to all those who have gone before us. For this I borrow words from the ancestral recognition statement. I am inspired by their vision and valour. Their lives continuously remind us that service is more important than success, people are more important than possessions, and principle is more important than power.

The list is endless, but when the focus is narrowed to sports and education, I have to single out one individual: Arthur Ashe was an athlete, activist, and scholar who did much more than just play the game of tennis. He spent a lifetime being passionate about sports and education. Rarely has anyone had the ability, resources and desire to lead such a struggle for change. After his playing days, Ashe was in no way obligated to do more, but he chose to. And he chose to prompt valuable social change when he announced his condition to the world in 1992, also announcing the Arthur Ashe Foundation for the defeat of AIDS. "I'm not a victim," Ashe said, "I'm a messenger." He was justly recognized by being the first sportsman in memory to receive the extraordinary tribute of lying in state.

Foreword

Kids can be the most innocent but also the meanest creatures on the face of the earth. Let me tell you a personal story. If you looked at me now, you would never know it, but I used to compete in gymnastics. I still remember my last competition as a gymnast representing my hometown of Windsor, Ontario, at the provincial championships. At the time, two gymnastic teams were operating in the city. I will refer to one team as the A team and the other as the B team. Now, the A team was much more established than the B team and had all the frills of a successful program—the finest coaches the city had to offer, uniforms and a generous sponsor. The B team, my team, on the other hand, was a new team that had not yet created an identity for itself. As a result, our practice times, facilities and the like were all second-rate compared to those of the A team, but that did not deter us from competing and training just as hard. In fact, most of us hoped to someday be a part of the A team. However, for me that thought quickly disappeared one day.

It was perhaps my rudest awakening as a Black athlete. Although it came at the innocent age of twelve, the experience still makes me shake my head in disbelief. It all began with a phone call from my coach, telling me I had qualified for the provincial championships. That was the good news. The bad news was I was the only one from the B team who had done so. After thinking about it and discussing it with my parents, we all felt that it was too good of an opportunity to pass up. Although my parents couldn't make it to the championships, which were being held in Ottawa, about a six-hour drive away, they gave me a send-off that left me as high as a kite. My coach could not make it to the competition either and had arranged a ride for me with the A team. I was instructed to meet them at Central Park at 6:30 a.m., which I did, and that is when the problems began.

Clearly I was an outsider. No one volunteered to take me in their car. This after the other fellows had been wooed to cars of parents driving. I had never in my young life felt so uncomfortable. I honestly did not know what to do, so I just stood there hoping someone would notice. Luckily, someone did notice and asked if I would like to ride with them. I will call her Mrs. Green. Her decision to ask me to ride in their car was not a popular one. In fact, her son became so agitated that she had to pull him over to the side and talk to him privately. But it was too little, too late; the damage was done. I still recall him telling his friends he didn't "want no coon" in his car and pleading with his mother, "Why, oh why, do we have to take him?" In fact, some of the other boys who were to ride in the same car threatened to ride with someone else if I came along. As it turned out, the only room left in their station wagon was at the back with the luggage. At the time, as far as I was concerned, the roof of the car would have been okay. But being at the back wasn't so bad; it allowed me to put on my headphones and shed a few tears without drawing attention to myself. The six-hour car ride seemed like twelve hours, especially when the other boys didn't even attempt to include me in their conversation. And if it wasn't for Mrs. Green shouting the occasional, "How you doing back there?" I probably wouldn't have said a word. Even when we stopped for food and fuel, I was on my own. The A team members were a tight-knit group who didn't give me the time of day.

When we finally reached our destination and were given our room assignments, I was on my own again. Now part of that must have come from the fact that I was the only one from the B team, and the A team had had room assignments before I arrived. But part of me thinks the skin I'm in didn't help either. That night all the members of the team gathered for dinner. I overheard their coach saying he would call the rooms and tell everyone what time they would be meeting in the morning. I never did get that call, which led me to believe they might forget me. After spending the night in a room by myself, tossing and turning and contemplating whether to call home (which I decided not to do out of fear that my parents would be on the next plane and make a scene any twelve-year-old would be embarrassed about), I got dressed and went down to the lobby at about 5:30 a.m. and waited. The coaches, parents and gymnasts arrived in the lobby at about 7:30 a.m. and coyly asked where I had been. Like they really cared.

It didn't take long for me to notice that I was the only Black gymnast competing in the championships. I'm not sure if it made a difference, but it was by far my worst performance. It was ironic that while competing I was positioned right after a member of the A team, which meant the opportunity to give me a little applause and wave the hometown banner was there if they wanted to. They certainly made some noise for Bobby, but my routine ended to utter silence. Not even a clap? Even today, as I reflect back on my days as an athlete and all the lessons I have learned through sports, I cannot help wondering if the skin I'm in has been a major factor.

The study of sport takes us to the heart of critical issues of culture and society, and into many aspects of the relationship between race and sport.

I am interested in Black youth and sports because of the significant role sports has played in my own life. Sports has helped me to organize my sense of self, my understanding of the world and the way I spend much of my leisure time. I bring to this book a background in both amateur and professional football. I was a Black student athlete on a football scholarship, and I excelled both academically and athletically. In my experience, sports function as a source of discipline and self-esteem, qualities that contribute to lifelong success. Thus I believe sport participation can have a positive impact on many aspects of one's life.

My interest in this area is also a result of my daily interactions with Black youth as an educator, coach and friend. Many of these youths have articulated a desire to pursue a professional sports career above all else. However, when sport participation becomes the central interest in a student's life, the situation can become problematic. This common problem, combined with the academic underachievement of Black youth in public schools, has prompted me to write this book.

Many of the Black youth I have worked with are bright, articulate, energetic and socially adept, but still they are neglected by the mainstream educational system at all levels. Educators are aware of the factors that lead to academic success, yet many continue practices that may be detrimental to their students.

Introduction

The image of the Black male as a savage, happy-go-lucky, dumb brute nigger was born out of the colonization of Africans and slavery. These images have travelled through time with the assistance of the mass media and have influenced attitudes and behaviours towards Black people. Hollywood's image of Tarzan—a lone White man who fully controls and dominates a land occupied by Blacks—didn't help either. Not only was Tarzan able to master Africa, but as King of the Jungle he knew more about the ways of the land than the Africans themselves, or at least that is what Hollywood would lead us to believe. These images continue to have damaging effects on Blacks and on the way we are perceived by society at large.

Not even in the realm of sport, the oft-cited domain of Black dominance, can we escape this image. Indeed, Blacks are highly represented on the field and in the arenas, but the front office and the positions of ownership are predominantly White. And the popularity and multimillion-dollar contracts that many Black athletes enjoy do not translate into the political and economic power required to produce the changes needed for sports and society to achieve equality for all. Unfortunately, it has long been the case that Whites have been able to acknowledge the athletic excellence of Blacks without giving up prejudices in other areas. Thus the greater sociological effect of this supposedly colour-blind celebrity and marketing revolution is virtually nil. That is shameful but does not come as a big surprise when one considers that, long before the word "crossover" was coined, Duke Ellington, Louis Armstrong, Billie Holiday and other black musicians were the rage of upper-class White society. "Come play for us, but just use the back door."

What about the recent trend of White American sports organizers to limit the number of Kenyans who may participate in American running events, reasoning that it is our country, our event and our money? Although Black athletes are the foundation of professional and amateur sports such as baseball, basketball, football, boxing, and track and field, the master-servant mentality still exists on the part of owners. Like slaves, the athletes are only to exhibit their physical skills when the owners say so.

This book confronts issues such as these, and it also reflects on provocative and controversial assertions, like those put forth by *Darwin's Athletes* author John Hoberman (1997), who digs up historical data to show that the link between race and athletic success stems from cultural conditioning. Hoberman uses historical examples to show that the Black athlete is not a biological phenomenon but rather a product of cultural circumstances. He argues that sports is an entrapment for Black men which turns them into commercial commodities within a power structure controlled by Whites. Those images still play into the hands of racists who claim that Blacks are physically superior but intellectually inferior.

The evolution of nationalities in boxing exhibits the importance of culture in sport. The first boxers were Irish immigrants who had come to the New World seeking a better life. They were poor, from Irish slums. As time moved on, Irish immigrants began to work their way up the social ladder and out of the boxing world. Then, as a wave of Italian and Jewish immigrants came to the United States, the nationality of boxing changed. And finally, once they became socially mobile, Blacks inhabited the ghettos. Today, Blacks dominate the poor inner city and also control the boxing world.

Much like Hoberman, I will argue that sport participation has become the "essence" of Blackness and has led many Blacks to prize athleticism to such a degree that it renders almost all other achievements meaningless. This condition has been brought on by a traumatic history and racism. Where do we get this attitude from? Look no further than the schools, the media, Black parents, relatives and friends, who demand excellence on the playing field but not always in the classroom. A recent survey revealed that Black parents are four times more likely than White parents to believe their children are destined for a career as a pro athlete (Edwards 1992). We have bought into sport because it has worked for some. In a society where racism is so pervasive and soul-destroying, sport has inadvertently closed off other means to opportunity and social mobility.

But has sport also opened doors? Hoberman argues that, despite the off-field achievements of Black heroes such as Jackie Robinson, Muhammad Ali and Arthur Ashe, "the tragedy is that the black athlete can neither advance nor lead his race in the modern world."

Hoberman's work is thought-provoking and serves as a reminder that sport is an undeniable and inescapable influence in life. As never before, sport permeates our culture and captures our collective minds. Why else would two-thirds of Black males between the ages of twelve and nineteen— about twice the rate of their White counterparts—believe they can earn a living playing professional sports? We have a racially charged obsession that has been called the "Air Jordan Effect." This expression describes a fixation, in which the riches and fame of sport heroes such as Michael Jordan have caused a wildly disproportionate number of young Blacks to focus on sports at the expense of more realistic and productive career paths. The commercial success of Black athletes, according to

Hoberman, operates in tandem with peer-group pressure to underperform academically, as the seductive effect of Jordan and company offers children the fantasy of an alternate life.

I agree with some of Hoberman's assertions, particularly the notion that "the presence of large numbers of black athletes in the major sports appears to have persuaded almost everyone that the process of integration has been a success. This sense of closure is an illusion that is rooted in the fact not of racial equality but in a combination of black apathy and white public relations efforts" (1997: 29–30). Evidence of this lies in the public tribute paid to Jackie Robinson, which makes us all stop and wonder how much better things are today than they were for him. The bottom line, Hoberman says, and I agree, is that African Americans and Canadians have inherited, since the 1920s, the idea that sports can play a salvational role in their lives. There was a profound belief, and there continues to be a belief, that Black athletes can change the racist thinking of Whites. It just hasn't worked out that way. I do, however, take exception to Hoberman's beliefs that the Black middle class (which would include me) is shying away from tough commentary on race and sports, suggesting that we might be tormented by the apparent contradiction between being a professor and being a home boy who may still be concerned about the impression he makes on the basketball court. I hope this book addresses that! It would be crazy to suggest that Blacks as a people should give up the success we already have. Whose interest would that serve? Indeed, many Black youth use sports to negotiate the structural constraints of the school system and to counter the dominating and detrimental effects of inequality, racism and discrimination (Carrington 1983; Cashmore 1982a; Solomon 1992). Throughout this book I will explore what is right and what is wrong with sport, but never will I suggest that Black sport participation should end. The students in this study talk about how sports can be a means of coping with an alienating school system, of exercising control over their schooling process, of negotiating with school authorities and of achieving social and academic success (Dei 1994; James1990). And that is all good.

This book presents my studies of the school experience of Black male student athletes and the relationship between their athletic participation and their academic and career aspirations. I studied Black student athletes because there is a dearth of research in this area, and because of my deep concern about their underachievement in public education. This book investigates the impacts of being an athlete and being Black on educational achievement and career choice. In light of these findings, several specific recommendations are made for the improvement of Black students' academic performance, and strategies for making schools more inclusive are also examined. The influences of parents, schools, peer groups, environment and mass media are also considered.

The term "Black" has come under scrutiny because Blacks are actually a diverse group of people who have been lumped together on the basis of skin colour. The terms "African Canadian" and "African American" have emerged to acknowledge commonalities in historical and cultural backgrounds. I will use the term "Black," as the bulk of available literature is by American authors of the 1970s and 1980s, who used "Black." Further, the term "Black" captures the essential component of the racialization of Black youth in sport. Thus by "Black students" I mean students of African ancestry, who identify themselves as such.

The main goal of my study was to examine whether sport participation in high school for Black male student athletes was positively related to behaviours that enhance individual academic success and career aspirations. The study provided Black student athletes with an opportunity to articulate their experiences in sports and the effect on their academic success.

I chose a qualitative research methodology in order to characterize the experiences of the twenty-five Black male, high school athletes I interviewed. A quantative approach, that is, objective measurements of specific behaviours on predetermined scales, would not have yielded the inside understanding I was seeking in order to appreciate what it is like to be a Black male student athlete. The research questions addressed to the athletes focused on four issues: (1) academic aspirations, (2) career planning, (3) classroom and academic experiences and (4) attitudes towards self and others.

I also interviewed twenty-five male and female teachers and administrators, selected from diverse racial, ethnic and gender backgrounds. Their years of experience ranged from two to twenty-eight and their average years of experience was 12.8. The majority of educator participants came from the boards of education of North York (16), Toronto (4), Scarborough (3) and the City of York (2). The research questions addressed to the educators focused on six issues: (1) the representation of Black males in public high school sports, (2) the role of the school in sport participation, (3) the role of teachers in sport participation, (4) the role of students in sport participation, (5) the importance of sports to Black male youths and (6) the effects of sport participation on Black male, high school athletes' academic and career aspirations.

Although discussions may make reference to Blacks in Ontario, and in metropolitan Toronto in particular, these issues and concerns are common to other Black students in North America and Europe. It is important to note that my respondents are from working-class backgrounds. Other studies reveal that African Canadian students in the Toronto area tend to come from lower socioeconomic sectors of society (Cheng, Yau and

Zeigler 1993), and many of these working-class youth tend to see sport as a means of coping with school (Cashmore 1982a; Carrington 1983; James 1990; Solomon 1992).

A number of studies (Dei 1995; Solomon 1992; James 1990; Head 1975) on African Canadian youth in Toronto schools have discussed their educational problems and identified that sports play a very significant role in their schooling process. However, no study using the theoretical framework and methodology employed in this book has discussed how Black students have used sports to construct their academic and career aspirations. The narratives of the students and educators are sensitive and illuminating.

The success of *The Skin I'm In* will be measured by the extent to which it reveals the deep and pervasive effects of racism in sport on Black student athletes, and by how much it contributes to an understanding that teachers, the educational system, parents and fellow students should encourage a youth's performance in the classroom first and on the playing field second.

Chapter 1

Experiences of Black People in Canadian Society

In 1936, Black Canadian Fred Christie was refused service in a bar at the Forum, the Montreal hockey arena. He had ordered a beer but was told by the waiter that he couldn't be served. The police were called and he later decided to sue for damages. The case wound up in the Supreme Court of Canada in 1939, and the court decided that this kind of discrimination was permissible!

Canada has still not created a society which truly respects differences. In Canada, as in other societies built on conquest and immigration, the conquerors have the advantages, and the conquered and the newly arrived are placed at the bottom of the so-called opportunity structure.

Racism, as defined by Carl James (1995: 37), "is the uncritical acceptance of a negative social definition of a colonized or subordinate group typically identified by physical features. . . . These racialized groups are believed to lack certain abilities or characteristics, which in turn characterizes them as culturally and biologically inferior." This kind of racism exists in Canada, despite Canada's official policy on multiculturalism and tolerance, which recognizes the cultural diversity of Canada as a demographic reality. Canadian policy suggests that everyone will be treated equally, regardless of culture and ethnic origin, and given the opportunity to participate fully in Canadian life. This policy has led racial minorities to expect equal access to Canadian life and opportunities. However, in fact the policy pays generous grants to minorities to maintain their cultures and thereby ghettoizes them.

But have racial minorities in Canada been afforded any better opportunities in schooling than other racial minorities in Western democracies?

The present, well-documented crisis in Canadian education is personified for Black students. This crisis is revealed in part by statistical parameters, including low test scores, suspensions and dropout rates. For example, Toronto Board of Education studies over two decades showed that Black students were second to Aboriginals in being the most highly represented in basic level programs of study (Wright 1971; Deosaran 1976; Cheng, Yau and Zeigler 1993). In a 1991 high school survey of a Toronto area board of education, it was revealed that African Canadian youth were not accumulating credits as well as other students were. It was shown that 36 percent of Black students were at risk of dropping out because of failure to gather sufficient credits to graduate in six years— this compared with 26 percent for Whites and 18 percent for Asians (Cheng 1995). The board of education's study of high school students who had enrolled in 1987 also revealed that, by 1991, 42 percent of the Black students (compared to 33 percent of the overall population) had dropped out of school. The 1994 Royal Commission on Learning confirmed these findings and concluded that there is a need for concern about the school participation and achievement of Black students.

The students and educators I interviewed report a general lack of sensitivity on the part of teachers and coaches to the individual and sociocultural needs of Black students. In particular, low expectations, stereotypes about Black students, prejudicial beliefs about intelligence, and a general lack of support are reported to characterize educators' attitudes.

Given the extent of discrimination in schools and the labour market, and the lack of other opportunities to achieve respect and dignity, it is understandable that Black male students would pursue athletic success. Sport is a very important part of the lives of the informants and is an area in which they can excel and be recognized. Several researchers have indicated that participation in sport is an esteem-building activity that develops values of discipline, goal setting and persistence that carry over to the classroom. This appears to be true for my informants as well. The young men in this study revealed the importance of sports to them as a motivator, emotional outlet and source of help in financing university. However, inordinate focus on sport also detracted from study time and set up unrealistic career expectations.

Public schools, as social institutions, are under pressure to respond to significant shifts in the way that we see society and the way we treat individuals as groups in society. Central to the concept of societal justice is the belief that all should have an equal chance to succeed in the common school system. But opinions as to what an equal chance means, and to whom these chances should be extended, have changed substantially over time. Equality of educational opportunity, at least theoretically, has been extended to include minorities and women. The emphasis has shifted from the provision of formal or legal equality of opportunity to the requirement that educational institutions take active or affirmative steps to ensure the equal treatment of different groups. Underlying this shift in emphasis is the emergence of a concept of equality of opportunity measured by equality of results. Educational institutions are held partly accountable for gross differences in the attendance or success rates of different groups and are expected to take measures to reduce those differences.

It has been accepted that one of the goals of education is to prepare individuals for the work world, a European model which comes out of a history of male domination and authority. For individuals to be successful, they must learn behaviours that meet the demands of the economic system. Traditional education has supported this goal and has reproduced it with each generation.

The teacher has the responsibility to liberate the voice of the student and enable him or her to relate to information from the perspective of his or her own experience. Learning can then become a liberating, personal and individual experience. This approach to learning leaves room for minority students to find their own identities. Finding, reinforcing and learning through one's cultural identity leads to strong self-esteem and positive self-expectations. It is difficult to find one's own voice when history, literature and cultural expectations have unfamiliar faces and voices. Pride in one's roots is essential to finding one's voice.

Historically, school systems have tended to reflect the belief that a nation is composed of one language, one people, one culture, one religion etc. Therefore, non-dominant group members were expected to conform or, through a "melting pot" process, become integrated into the dominant culture. The failure of the "melting pot" process and the resulting inequities have led to an increased acceptance of diversity as a positive element in education.

The Unique History of Black People in Canada

It is important to recognize that Black people have a unique history in Canada. Three facts stand out above all others: Blacks came to this country from Africa and not from Europe; they came in chains; and they have been subjected to systemic exclusion from participation and influence in the major institutions of this society even to the present time. The vestiges of the Black heritage—the experience of slavery, the mix of cultures, the transition to urban communities and the persistence of racism—play important roles in an understanding of contemporary Black experience.

In his book *Racial Discrimination in Canada: The Black Experience*, James Walker writes that from 1628, when the first enslaved African person was brought to Quebec, African people in Canada were associated with slavery, and therefore with a subordinate role in society. Following the British conquest, more Black slaves entered Canada and enslavement became more exclusively a Black condition (1985: 8).

When Upper Canada was founded in 1792, nine members of the appointed upper Legislative Council either owned enslaved Africans or were members of slave-owning families. In the elected lower Legislative

Assembly, six of the original sixteen members owned enslaved Africans. Although slavery was never as strong an economic force in the northern British colonies as it was in the southern former colonies, the enslavement of African children, women and men was integral to the development of colonial society in British North America. Enslaved Africans, such as Marie-Joseph-Angelique in Montreal in 1734, rebelled against their enslavement and sought refuge in the United States (Walker 1985).

Through the first half of the 1800s, tens of thousands of enslaved African children, women and men emancipated themselves from slavery in the southern United States and fled north, many thousands seeking refuge in Canada. Especially after the Fugitive Slave Act of 1850 and the U.S. Supreme Court's decision that African Americans had no rights a White person was bound to respect, many more thousands of "free" Black people in northern cities fled to Canada. Others, closer to Mexico, fled for safety there.

Walker observes that:

> The Underground Railroad fostered a myth that the North Star led not just out of slavery, but into freedom, equality and participation in Canadian life. . . . The North Star myth entered the Canadian identity and became a major feature distinguishing Canadians from Americans: only south of the border were Blacks subjected to violence, denied their citizenship rights, forced into residential ghettoes. . . . The North Star myth was a liability for Canada, for it prevented any sincere examination of the situation faced by Blacks and other "visible minorities." It allowed Canadians to believe that Canada had no "race problem," that Canadian Blacks were satisfied with conditions here, that there was no cause for concern or for corrective action (1985: 6–7).

Imagine the look on faces across the Great White North when the headlines in the morning newspaper read "Canada as racist as the USA," that quote coming from Donovan Bailey. Donovan Bailey and Bruny Surin had spoken with *Sports Illustrated* about their views on race and Canadian society. This comment was made in relation to the way Ben Johnson was treated when he lost his gold medal in the Seoul Olympics in 1988 after he tested positive for steroids.

The unfortunate reality is that Canada is still a racist society.

Chapter 2

Blacks in Sport

We have raped a generation of young Black athletes. We have taken kids and sold them on bouncing a ball and running with a football and that being able to do certain things athletically was going to be an end in itself. We cannot afford to do that to another generation.
—Joe Paterno, Head Football Coach, Penn State University

Popular opinion holds that to succeed in sport is to succeed in life, and that sport develops desirable character traits and values. Some suggest sport is an inspiration for Black athletes. On the other side of the debate is the contention that the educational advantages and social mobility opportunities accrued from sport are minimal (McElroy 1980), if not dysfunctional for Black male youth (Gaston 1986).

Today, more than ever, a new code of ethics is needed within sport. It is time for educators to insist that academics come first. Take Spike Lee's film, "He Got Game," for example. A high school basketball phenom, Jesus, is wined and dined by recruiters, showered with cash and women and fed a steady diet of pending glory and mega paydays. The problem is there is no mention of education.

We as a society ask for this. We even set aside a major segment of our daily newspaper and television programming to highlight athletic achievement. We don't do that for science fair winners, nor do we see college scouts visiting inner-city school math classes the way they visit basketball practices. The real champions in our society are not those who run with an idea, but those who run with a ball. This kind of thinking is perpetuated not only by Whites but by Blacks as well. Evidence lies in the self-stereotyping that leads many Black youth to ridicule their peers as "brainiacs" or acting White for opening a book. When the Black Olympic gold medalist sprinter Lee Evans said in 1981, "We were simply bred for physical qualities," he was not saying anything different than what O.J. Simpson, Carl Lewis, Hall of Fame baseballer Joe Morgan, current baseball star Barry Bonds or Jimmy the Greek have said. Ironically, White supremacists and Black supremacists both emphasize Black athletic superiority. The only difference is that while Black supremacists cite alleged Black biological superiority as evidence of a more general superiority,

White supremacists cite it as evidence of lower intelligence of a more animal nature. None of these assertions are that far removed from the claims of Charles Darwin, who once speculated that an "animal possessing great size, strength, and ferocity" would probably fail to evolve the "higher mental qualities" necessary for civilized life.

It seems that Whites have long been fascinated with the Black body, and the only thing that has changed is the interpretation. In the nineteenth century, speculation centred on the stunted Negro. Doctors noted that Black people responded badly to physical stress and supposedly had weak lungs and less blood than was good for a person. Hoberman (1997) reminds us about the Tuskegee airmen, the all-Black aviation team that was nearly prevented from flying combat missions during World War II. He says that the concept that Blacks were "physiologically unsuited for military aviation" was argued on the basis that Blacks carry the sickle cell trait and that this disorder could endanger the carrier and fellow crew members under "hypoxic conditions." Hoberman points out that the effects of this belief in the biological inferiority of Blacks persisted until 1981, when the U.S. Air Force modified its policies.

The idea that Blacks were physically feeble became harder to sustain as Black success in sports mounted. In fact, the sporting success of Black athletes began an obsession with Black physical superiority. Even before Jesse Owens won his four gold medals at the 1936 Olympics, scientists had measured his heel bone to see if it was longer than his competitors— it wasn't. And one of Owen's White coaches later wrote: "The Negro excels in the events he does because he is closer to the primitive than the white man" (Hoberman 1997: 67).

More recently, Charles Murray and Richard Hernstein, authors of the *The Bell Curve* (1996), cite "the dominance of many Black athletes" as the single Black achievement they can think of. And Canadian psychologist Phillip Rushton, in an interview on the "Geraldo Rivera Show," said, "Even if you take something like athletic ability or sexuality, it's a trade-off: more brains or more penis. You can't have everything."

All this becomes problematic when educators bring this racist ideology into the classroom and start believing that Black kids are simply not able to succeed academically, and that sports is their best shot. Thus aspiring to "be like Mike," kids spend countless hours mastering their dribbling and shooting skills with little thought to their futures after their sports days are done. Their heads are stuffed with thoughts of "Hoop Dreams," when the reality is they most likely will never get those big paydays playing ball games. The fact is, the chance of any Black high school athlete making it in any professional sport is only about one in 15,000. Becoming a pro has the same probability as flipping a coin fifteen times and always getting heads—perhaps not impossible, but extremely remote. I was stunned when eighteen out of twenty Black kids in a counselling group four other teachers and I were running, a group called Boys to Men, identified sport as their future occupation. What floored me was that most of these kids had never played on a school team or in any kind of organized sport league, but somehow they thought they would be playing in the big leagues. In fact, one kid thought he would make it by playing nerf basketball in his bedroom for three hours at night! That experience prompted me to write and produce a five-minute video called "No J (No Job)," which tells the tale of a fallen basketball star who can't get a job.

As a Louisana high school coach put it in 1968, "A White kid tries to become President of the United States, and all the skills and knowledge he picks up on the way can be used in a thousand different jobs. A Black kid tries to become Willie Mays, and all the tools he picks up are useless to him if he doesn't become Willie Mays" (Hutchinson 1998). The fact of the matter is that only 2.3 percent, or 215, of the 9,500 college football seniors will be drafted into the National Football League (NFL). And the odds are 250 to one that a college basketball player will ever wear a National Basketball Association (NBA) jersey.

The chances for Blacks to own, run, manage or work in any capacity for pro teams are also dim. As of 1998, there were no Black football, baseball or basketball professional team owners and very few Black managers and football coaches. There was one Black team doctor in baseball, none in football, and only a handful of Black team trainers in all the sports combined. Making things worse is the report card on the graduation rates for Black student athletes at fifty Division 1 National Collegiate Athletic Association (NCAA) schools during the 1990s (Lapchick 1996). This report revealed that the majority of these athletes brought fame and fortune to their schools. It almost appears that college athletic departments have created modern-day plantations, with the alumni as the masters, the coach as the well-paid overseer and the Black athletes as the slaves. Hoberman (1997: 39) makes the same kind of analogy. He points out that, despite the huge sums of money that Black pro players such as Dennis Rodman can earn in salaries and endorsements, the arrangement that wins them these benefits is still part of the legacy of slavery and Jim Crow racism. Put Black players on the court or playing field and watch them perform for their White managers, owners, coaches and fans; take them off, and these Blacks must still face the ravages of racism.

So what should we do? Keeping track of graduation rates is a waste of time. Those numbers only reveal how many athletes receive a degree, not how many receive an education. Many Black athletes stroll through three or four years at college and still emerge without an education, with a curriculum filled with pottery, basket weaving and general courses.

I certainly would never suggest that Blacks should stop participating in sport. The African American community should not discourage its youth from sport participation, for it has benefited the community in many ways. As Harry Edwards (1983) says, "On a spiritual level, the performances of outstanding black athletes have bolstered black pride and self-esteem. On a practical level, sports have been means to higher education opportunities for many black youths . . . who have moved on to establish productive careers in other fields. Further, by virtue of their enormous accomplishments in sport, black athletes have demonstrated that the greatest obstacle to black achievement in all the areas of American life has not been lack of capacity or competitiveness, but a lack of opportunity."

Research findings have consistently shown that sport participation increases educational aspirations, especially for those students who would otherwise not view them as possible. A 1989 study shows that Black males from urban high schools were four times more likely to work towards a bachelor's degree than their non-athletic counterparts. The reasons for the increase in educational aspirations among Black student athletes has been explained in two theories (Howell, Miracle and Rees, 1990). The "personal contact" hypothesis theorizes that students gain positive contacts through sports. They achieve access to the school's elite crowd which is usually composed of children of higher socioeconomic status. And these children view college as the obvious path after graduation and instill these values in their friends. Alternatively, the "athletic involvement helps academic success" argument asserts that sports improves students' self-concepts, thereby leading them to develop higher aspirations for themselves, including a university career.

But even that argument is questionable when you consider that NCAA universities give away more than $600 million in athletic scholarships each year. The pool for all other awards, including minority scholarships and merit-based grants, is $49.7 billion. The education a college athlete receives is no doubt beneficial. And Black athletes have a slightly better chance of graduating from college than non-Black athletes (Lapchick 1996).

The Influence of Sport on Children and Youth

Schools today are populated by children and youth with views different from their teachers, principals, parents, guardians and caregivers. Some of these differences can be attributed to the emergence of contemporary agents of socialization and their effects upon the young. In the past, the primary agents of socialization in Western countries were the family, the church and the school. Today these institutions share their socialization functions with popular music, television, peer groups and sports.

Sports in particular have a strong influence on youth. Sport has become a major industry, a highly visible business that attracts millions of observers. It is an arena of social life packed with the power of symbolism. For instance, sports can reinforce the idea that hard work and natural ability are all that is needed to achieve success, that even those from humble origins, regardless of race, may achieve equal opportunity. And, as we have seen, they may also reinforce beliefs that innate physical and psychological differences exist between the races and that these account for the scarcity of Blacks in leadership positions on and off the field.

Blacks have been struggling for equality for many years. Yet only in sports and entertainment can it be said (with some reservations) that Blacks have made considerable progress. As a result of the visibility and performance of Black athletes, and the pride taken in their accomplishments, sports has been assigned a special significance. But does participation in sports help or hinder the Black male student athlete? Those who argue that sports benefit Black male student athletes point to the relatively colour-blind nature of athletic participation. Sport is viewed as one of the few meritocracies.

On a football field, skin colour is less important than speed, strength and skill. Despite making up only 13 percent of the population and about 4 percent of the student body at the predominantly White Division 1 universities in the United States, Black student athletes make up 37 percent of the football players, 33 percent of the women's basketball players and 56 percent of the men's basketball players (Center for the Study of Athletics 1989: 7–11). Part of the "sports provide opportunities" theory is that sports provide one of the few legal opportunities for social mobility to Blacks who are able to exploit the system; sports provide educational and career opportunities to Black student athletes from under-privileged backgrounds which are often beyond the reach of some of their more academically gifted but less athletically endowed Black classmates.

Another view suggests involvement in sport has positive consequences for participants and society as a whole. Among the positive aspects associated with sport is its function as a transmitter of social values. Through athletic participation, it is argued, one learns not only how to play a specific sport but also how to play the game of life. Sport presumably transmits, among other values, the importance of hard work, character development and team work, values that are complementary to those necessary for success in academic life. Sport, therefore, has been traditionally viewed as beneficial to the achievement of academic goals.

Another view contends that sports have been detrimental to Black student athletes, particularly those who have not made it to the professional level. In this argument, emphasis is placed on the limited opportunities that many Black student athletes will face when career aspirations are limited to playing professional sports. For example, a Black high school football player has a two in forty-three chance of playing for a Division 1 university football team. His chance of playing in the NFL is one in 6,318. A Black male high school basketball player has about a one in 130 chance of playing for a Division 1 basketball team and the odds are 10,345 to one against his playing in the NBA (Lapchick 1991). Further, only one of four Black Division 1 athletes have graduated from their university five years after arrival (NCAA 1991).

Coleman (1961) expressed his concern that high schools give the appearance of being organized around sport rather than academics, as indicated by the visibility of symbols of athletic achievements (for example, displays of athletic trophies in school lobbies) and the relative invisibility of symbols of academic accomplishments (for example, an absence of displays of school awards). It is significant to note that although Coleman's concerns date from 1961, little has changed in appearance and athletes are still accorded higher status in high school than scholars.

Informants from my study concur. For example, Lon said:

> You get enough respect for playing ball. That's just the way it is, people respect you if you have a game. I don't know of anything that has the same respect as ball (July 29, 1994).

Nigel:

> You get a lot of attention if you're good. I think everyone sees that and strives for it. I know school is important and everything, but nobody asks you out to lunch or gives you stuff for being on the honour roll (May 31, 1994).

Arnold:

> Black people love an athlete. You get a lot of favours. Everybody sees that and tries to get some of it. Just go to a ball game and watch how the people who have a good game are treated. Everybody wants to stay friends with you because when you make it they can say they know you (June 4, 1994).

The notion of sport as a threat to academics complements the concept of the athlete as an individual uninterested in studying. This stereotype holds that time and energy spent on athletics is time and energy taken away from the pursuit of academic concerns, because athletic excellence requires an enormous amount of time and energy. This stereotype has given rise to the dominant ideology that athletes are poor students. The phrase "dumb jock" is evidence of this ideology.

Those who support this perspective suggest that the lure of sports distracts athletes from other, more stable avenues of social success such as academic excellence. The sports establishment benefits from Black athletes' skill and labour by providing the illusion of an opportunity for fame, fortune and education. However, in the end, the majority of Black student athletes are exploited without compensation for their services (Sellers 1992). Harry Edwards sums up this argument:

> This channelling process tragically leads millions of Blacks to pursue a goal that is foredoomed to elude all but an insignificant few. . . . The impact of what would otherwise be personal career tragedies reverberates throughout Black society, both because of the tremendous proportion of Black youth channelled into sport and the fact that serious sport involvement often dictates neglect of other important spheres of development. Further, the skills cultivated through sport are utterly worthless beyond the sport realm (1979: 119).

Coakley (1986: 25) summarizes the traditional arguments for and against sport participation in the following manner:

> Arguments for sport participation:
> * Involves students in school activities and increases interest in academic activities
> * Builds the responsibility, achievement orientation and physical vigour required for adult participation in society
> * Stimulates interests in physical activities among all students in the school
> * Generates unity and spirit in the school
> * Promotes parental, alumni and community support for all sport programs.
>
> Arguments against sport participation:
> * Distracts the attention of students away from academic activities
> * Perpetuates dependence and immaturity; relegates most students to the role of spectator rather than participant
> * Creates a superficial, transitory spirit subverting the educational goals of the school
> * Deprives educational programs of resources, facilities, staff and community support.

My informants talked about the positive impacts that sports have had on their lives. Many Black student athletes mentioned the desirable character traits they have developed through sport participation, while others suggested that sports have made them look to their futures. Ev:

> It has kept me focused. All my coaches have talked about discipline and staying away from trouble, and that has influenced me so much. The sports have influenced me to keep working hard and to stay in school. I haven't dropped out. I'm taking advanced level courses and doing well. I think sports have a lot to do with that (May 30, 1994).

Richard spoke of the effects of sport participation on his life and the desirable character traits sports have helped him develop:

> To tell you the truth, I never used to think about college or university. Sports have made me look to the future more, because if I want to go on, I'm going to have to go to college or university. Sports have made me a better person. They have taught me discipline—getting to class on time, doing homework, teaching you manners—all kinds of stuff. If I want to keep running, I have to stay in school and that is positive (June 23, 1994).

Kirk:

> Sports will make me the man that I want to become. I know for sure that as long as I am playing sports I'm happy and goal-oriented. It keeps me on track and keeps me striving. The self-discipline that I have learned is phenomenal. I want a lot of things out of life and I really believe I will achieve them because of my sport participation background. What I have difficulty with, people will help me with, as long as I'm playing. When that's done, a lot of doors will be shut. It's my job to get all I can while I can (June 1, 1994).

Damion:

> It has been very positive for me. I feel better about myself what I'm doing and the goals I have. I never used to see past tomorrow, but now as an athlete I have to look to the future and my future involves school. Not only to keep playing, but also being around people heading in that direction makes you realize it is very important. I want a good life and sports has made me realize I can have it (July 6, 1994).

Cecil:

> I don't know where I would be. I'd probably be hanging out. Sports have brought order to my life. I just have a better understanding of what it takes to make it and sports are responsible for that. The discipline, the dedication to be a successful athlete are things that will make me successful in whatever I do. I don't do drugs. I don't drink. I don't stay out late. I think I'm making good decisions about my life. I'd be lying if I didn't say sports have played a big part in that (July 5, 1994).

The debate over the value of sports to the Black student athlete rests on the question:

> What happens to Black student athletes once their athletic career ends? Do their stories read like Kevin Ross or do they read like Thomas LaVeist?
>
> Kevin Ross was a basketball player at Creighton University. Ross spent four years at Creighton as a member of the basketball team and a member of the student body. However, after his athletic eligibility was exhausted and he was unable to succeed with an NBA team, he found himself a functional illiterate with only 70 credit hours of college course work. He made headlines by enroling in the Marva Collins Westside Preparatory School in Chicago, beginning as a fifth grader. At present Kevin Ross is suing Creighton University.
>
> Thomas LaVeist grew up in a rough section of Brooklyn. Although very intelligent, LaVeist never truly applied himself during his high school days. He was a student with "A" ability, but he performed at "C" level. He was fortunate enough to receive a football scholarship from the University of Maryland— Eastern Shore. While at UMES, LaVeist became a more diligent student. He went on to receive a Ph.D. in medical sociology. Today, Dr. Thomas LaVeist is a very successful professor at the John Hopkins University School of Public Health, as well as the President of the Alexandria Consortium, a prominent consulting firm. Dr. LaVeist credits much of his success to the educational opportunity he received. Because of his poor high school academic record, and his family's financial situation, he would never have been able to go to college without an athletic scholarship (Lapchick 1991: 259)

An other important question is: How and why do some people become involved in sports while others do not? Early studies indicate that most people who become involved in sports have been influenced by others who served as role models or in some way reinforced the athletic role behaviour. They point to the family as being generally responsible for early sport socialization. Parents who have positive evaluations of sports tend to produce children who view sports positively. One of the ways the Black community encourages participation in and valuation of sport for its members is through family support.

As Damion suggests:

> I think our community, the Black community, pushes kids into sports. If you're an athlete, everyone seems to respect you. You get so much further if you're an athlete. Parents know that sports are a way out for us and they push us into it. They've been through it and they know how hard it is out there. They know that ball could be the ticket out (July 6, 1994).

Gary, a science and math teacher who has been teaching for four years, commented on the impact of role models and the status given to athletes:

> If you're a good athlete, it is very prestigious. You get instant status, much more than if you receive an academic scholarship. Kids see that and channel their efforts into areas where it appears to be the most profitable (August 15, 1994).

According to Edwards (1984), sport is rewarded more and earlier by Black families than are other activities.

Sport permeates our society. As a result, it has significant influence on the lives of individuals and the Black male student athlete is no exception. In fact, many Black student athletes see athletics as a means of upward social mobility, resulting in the pursuit of "the dream" of becoming a superstar. However, allegiance to such a dream can become a major liability for many young Black male student athletes, especially those with athletic ability who attempt to model their behaviour in such a way that they become committed to sport as a vocation.

A Brief History of Blacks in U.S and Canadian Sport

Any discussion of the history of Blacks in modern sport has to start with the talented athletes who toiled in relative obscurity in the Negro baseball leagues.

Segregated baseball lasted sixty years, from 1887 when Adrian "Cap"

Anson, the Babe Ruth of his day, tried to order a Black opponent off the field, until 1947 when Jackie Robinson took his place in the infield at Ebbets Field in Brooklyn. During that time, many of the most gifted players ever to play the game did so virtually unnoticed. Some of these great players, such as Satchel Paige and Roy Campanella, benefited from Jackie Robinson's historic move, but many others, such as Josh Gibson, John Henry Lloyd, "Smoky Joe" Williams and James Thomas "Cool Papa" Bell, missed out.

Blacks have played baseball on "White teams" since the game's beginnings in the mid-nineteenth century. They can track their professional ties within the sport to John "Bud" Fowler who played briefly for a White professional team in New Castle but was eventually forced to admit that "my skin colour is against me." The second Black professional to play on a racially mixed team was Moses Fleetwood Walker, who played for Toledo in the American Association in 1893. The International League also produced pitcher George Stovey, a Black Canadian who won thirty-three games for Newark in one year and only lost four. The White leagues eventually passed a rule banning Black players, and many Black players joined the Cuban Giants, the first Black major league–calibre professional team.

My favourite Black player is Oscar Charleston, a tough ex-soldier who hit with power, ran with Ty Cobb's speed and played a sensational centre field. Twice he led the Negro National League in both home runs and stolen bases. He was reportedly strong enough to loosen a baseball's cover with one hand, and fearless enough to snatch the hood from the head of a Ku Klux Klansman. He was sometimes called "the Black Cobb," but those who saw both men play disagreed; Cobb, they said, was "the White Charleston."

Because accurate statistics are lacking, it is hard to say just how good these players were, but based on their exhibition play against their White professional counterparts, it is clear they were exceptional. Black teams opposed White professional teams in more than four hundred games between the 1890s and 1947 and came away winners 60 percent of the time. White players such as Babe Ruth and Ty Cobb were glad to make extra money in games against Blacks.

According to Wiggins (1991), during the latter half of the nineteenth century, sport was not of primary importance to Black student athletes; they were more concerned about academic success. Many of these student athletes were from upper-middle-class families and had attended private academies, prestigious public schools or Black colleges in the South. Still, few schools even in the North accepted them on their athletic teams. The U.S. Military Academy and U.S. Naval Academy (Army and Navy), Catholic schools such as Notre Dame, and Ivy League schools such as

Princeton and Yale all shunned Black athletes, if not Blacks altogether. Athletic ability and a predisposition for academic success meant nothing to coaches and administrators if the athletes were not White.

During the next few decades, intercollegiate sport provided a few more opportunities for Blacks to participate, mostly in football and track and field. A large number of northern schools had Blacks on their teams, but segregation still prevailed off the field. In many cases there was only one Black on the team (and few on campus). As Behee (1974) has noted, those who made varsity teams were "Superspades." They were expected to do more than simply participate in the team's success; they were expected to carry the team to victory. Wallis Ward is a shining example of a "Superspade." He scored thirteen of the University of Michigan's $18^{3/4}$ points to lead the team to victory over Illinois in the 1932 Butler Relays. Three years later, Jesse Owens scored forty of Ohio State's $40^{1/5}$ points in a win over U.C. Berkeley. Paul Robeson, the lone Black on campus at Rutgers, was an All-American in 1917 and 1918. They and other Blacks were expected to provide super performances to justify their presence on athletic teams at predominantly White colleges and universities.

Super performances notwithstanding, Blacks were often treated shabbily by their schools. Campus housing was off limits to most of them; they were refused service in restaurants and not allowed to stay at hotels with their White teammates, even in northern cities; and, most humiliatingly, they were kept out of both home and away games against southern teams. (When playing southern teams on the road, northern teams were expected to be gracious guests by keeping their Black players, who were considered offensive to southern Whites, off the field. When northern teams played at home against southern teams, they were expected to be gracious hosts by again keeping their Black players off the field.) The NCAA steered clear of these abominable practices, and the games went on as planned. However, players such as Robeson, an All-American for two years and a Phi Beta Kappa at Rutgers, had to watch from the sidelines as their football teams sought to uphold the honour of the school without them (Wiggins 1989).

While a few Blacks, such as Robeson, Ward, Fritz Pollard and "Duke" Slater, were found in football programs in the North, most were barred from athletic activities that required interracial contact. Until the 1930s, most of the Black participation occurred in track and field. According to Behee (1974), between one hundred and two hundred Black athletes were competing for major colleges and universities at the time of the 1936 Olympics. Only later would football and basketball programs begin to accept Blacks in more than token roles.

Wiggins (1989) found that World War II brought about a number of changes in the status of Blacks. They, like others, had fought in Europe to eliminate Nazism, yet racism pervaded nearly every institution. Upon their return they, along with Black civilians, were prepared to fight for equality and integration at home.

After the war, several factors combined to greatly increase the college attendance rates of Blacks. Congress created the G.I. Bill, which provided funds for the post-secondary education of returning servicemen. This allowed many people to attend college who would otherwise have lacked the finances to do so. More than one-fourth of the students registered at colleges and universities in 1945–46 were veterans of World War II (Andrews 1984). Many Blacks were among the beneficiaries of the G.I. Bill (Green 1982); in some instances, they were former athletes who, in addition to furthering their education, were interested in participating in collegiate sports (Wiggins 1989).

President Truman appointed an interracial committee to investigate problems in higher education and to further opportunities for minorities (Franklin and Moss 1988). Its recommendations made discrimination at colleges and universities a national issue (Wiggins 1991), and made college desegregation a more acceptable practice. Finally, after the war, professional sports—baseball, football and basketball—began to accept more Black players on their teams, and collegiate sport was moving in the same direction.

All of these factors, according to Wiggins (1989), resulted in the presence of more Blacks at predominantly White colleges and universities. Consequently, at a time when society was more receptive to Blacks, at least at the level of secondary structural assimilation, there was also a larger pool of potential Black athletes available to collegiate athletic teams.

The change in racial attitudes in intercollegiate sport led to a new look in collegiate football. In 1944, two Blacks were selected to the *Look* magazine All-American team; however, no others were selected in the 1940s. But in the 1950s, fifteen Blacks made the magazine's All-American team (Behee 1974).

Basketball experienced similar changes. By 1948, 10 percent of the basketball programs at predominantly White colleges and universities had Blacks on their rosters; and one percent of all players at these schools were Black (Berghorn, Yetman and Hanna 1988). Although this was not a large number of Blacks, it was a sizeable increase from the pre–World War II figures. No Black basketball player was named to *Look* magazine's All-American team until 1952, but thereafter Blacks have been on every *Look* All-American team. Twenty-one made the team during the 1950s (Behee 1974). The Associated Press named five Blacks to the 1958 All-American team, the first of many times this has happened since.

As more Blacks participated in intercollegiate sport, the "Superspade" requirement was dropped. However, a disproportionate number of Blacks were rookies of the year, conference most valuable players and All-Americans. They, more than their White peers, were still expected to turn in stellar performances in return for their athletic scholarships.

The desegregation of collegiate sports did not mean the full integration of sport. Blacks in the 1940s and 1950s faced many of the same problems their predecessors had. For example, while their teammates were quartered in prestigious hotels, they were often left to seek lodging at the "Black YMCA" or with Black families in town. When the University of Cincinnati team travelled to Texas in 1959, Oscar Robertson, the star of the team, had to stay at a Black college while the rest were housed in Houston (Ashe 1988). Even when an entire team stayed at the same hotel, segregation was carried out through racial pairing in room assignments; Black and White players were seldom allowed to room together (Wiggins 1989). To the disappointment of Black athletes, the post-war period did not result in the collapse of discrimination in intercollegiate sport. Nevertheless, there were some changes in the attitudes of Whites towards Black athletes. Many conferences dropped racial bans (Rader 1990) and the gentleman's agreement (Behee 1974) that prohibited Black participation in basketball and football (although schools continued to set quotas on the number of Blacks permitted on a team). Some schools cancelled games with teams that refused to play against their Black players. More importantly, Black athletes were experiencing a change in "attitude" and demeanour; resistance to their maltreatment was growing. Discontent would soon turn into rebellious outbursts (Wiggins 1989).

During the latter part of the 1950s, Blacks showed their impatience with unfulfilled promises of full equality by participating in mass demonstrations. Through peaceful forms of civil disobedience, they demanded an end to discriminatory practices such as segregated seating on public transportation and the disenfranchisement of eligible Black voters. Participants in the protest were counselled not to retaliate against those who verbally and physically assaulted them. Instead, they were advised to "turn the other cheek." According to Wiggins (1989), they were often met by violent mobs, police clubs, attack dogs and the spray of fire hoses, but the demonstrators, for the most part, remained nonviolent.

As the decade of the 1960s began, a new weapon of peaceful protest was unleashed on southern businesses: sit-ins. In February 1960, four Black students who attended North Carolina A&T were refused coffee at a department store in Greensboro, North Carolina (Wiggins 1989). Their response was to sit and wait for service, thereby depriving the store of the opportunity to profit from service to other customers, while bringing attention to their grievance. Soon the sit-in movement spread all over the South.

At the same time, institutions of higher education in the South found themselves engaged in heated battles over the issue of desegregation. In 1962, it took a court order, deputy marshals and the National Guard to enrol James Meredith at the University of Mississippi. The next year, Governor George C. Wallace, in defiance of a court order, stood in the door of the University of Alabama to prevent Blacks from enrolling and attending classes. Wallace proclaimed segregation to be a way of life in the South; and it was an unstated but widely acknowledged component of most organizations in the nation (Wiggins 1989).

Although discrimination was a way of life in most institutions, many thought sport, particularly college sport, was exempt, and there seemed to be evidence to support this egalitarian notion. By 1962, Blacks' presence in collegiate basketball was comparable to their distribution in the general population (Berghorn, Yetman and Hanna 1988). Oscar Robertson was college basketball's player of the year in 1960 (for the third consecutive time), and by 1966, when Cazzie Russell was player of the year, the All-American first team was predominantly Black and would remain that way the rest of the decade. In 1963, Loyola of Illinois started four Black players, a practice unheard of at that time in college basketball, and won the national championship. The decade ended with Lew Alcindor (later known as Kareem Abdul-Jabbar), also a three-time college basketball player of the year, leading UCLA to its third straight national championship.

Similar feats were accomplished by Black athletes in other college sports. Many of the records in track and field, particularly in the sprints, hurdles, relays and long jump, belonged to Blacks. Bob Hayes, Jim Hines and Charlie Greene held the fastest times in the 100-yard dash in the 1960s. Tommie Smith topped the field in the 220-yard dash, Wyomia Tyus set records in the 100-yard and 100-metre dashes, and Wilma Rudolph did the same in the 200-metre dash. Lee Calhoun was the 120-yard hurdles champion, and Black men owned the records in the 400-metre and 1600-metre relays (Edwards 1969). Perhaps most impressively, at the 1968 Olympics, Bob Beamon set a record in the long jump that would last for more than twenty-two years. Blacks were an integral part of many of the top collegiate track and field programs.

Black presence on the football field was growing as well, as evidenced by the honours athletes were winning. In 1961, Syracuse's Ernie Davis became the first Black to win the Heisman Trophy. In the sixties, two others would follow: Mike Garrett and O.J. Simpson, both of USC. Other players such as Gale Sayers and Warren McVea accumulated impressive rushing and passing statistics (Harris 1991).

By the middle of the 1960s even southern teams had begun to welcome Black athletes. The Southeastern Conference (SEC), one of the premier athletic conferences in the South, integrated in 1967; other southern conferences, such as the Atlantic Coast and Southwest conferences, had desegregated already. It seemed that programs all over the country sought Black athletes. But these athletes understood that the attention, adulation and rewards they received from the athletic department were ephemeral. They still felt the sting of prejudice and exclusion that the Black athletes who preceded them had experienced. They began to perceive that "once their athletic abilities are impaired by their age or by injury, only the ghetto beckons and they are doomed once again to that faceless, hopeless, ignominious existence they had supposedly forever left behind them" (Edwards 1969: xxvii).

Black collegiate athletes began to rebel. They called for an end to stacking (intraracial competition for team positions), racial stereotyping, policing of social activities (including interracial dating) and other forms of discrimination in athletic programs (Spivey 1985). In some cases they adopted the tactics of the civil rights movement and staged peaceful demonstrations. Black athletes, and some White athletes, boycotted practices and banquets and refused to compete in events for organizations that discriminated against Blacks, such as the New York Athletic Club, which had discriminatory policies regarding accommodations. In other cases, Black athletes announced their intention to cancel, "by any means necessary," athletic contests staged by schools that mistreated them as students and/or athletes (Edwards 1969). By 1968, a movement among Black athletes to boycott the Olympic Games in Mexico appeared to be growing. Athletes were using athletics to bring about social change.

The proposed boycott of the 1968 Olympics never materialized; few prominent Black athletes declined to participate in the Games. However, the struggle for social equality by Black athletes and the willingness of some to sacrifice their athletic scholarships for the movement brought about changes in college sport. This was in part due to Tommie Smith and John Carlos, two American sprinters who had finished first and third, respectively, in a world record–setting 200-metre dash at the 1968 Mexico City Olympic Games. At the traditional awards ceremony, the two victorious athletes mounted the award podium shoeless, clad in sweatsuits and black stocking feet. Smith wore a Black scarf around his neck, Carlos a string of Mardi Gras beads. Both men and the silver medallist, Australian Peter Norman, displayed buttons reading "The Olympic Project for Human Rights." During the playing of the "Star-Spangled Banner," Smith and Carlos thrust black-loved fists in the air—Smith his right, Carlos his left. Smith described the significant of his actions to ABC's Howard Cosell:

> My raised right hand stood for the power in Black America. Carlos' raised left hand stood for the unity of Black America.

> Together they formed an arch of unity and power. The Black scarf around my neck stood for Black pride. The black socks with no shoes stood for Black poverty in racist America. The totality of our effort was the regaining of Black dignity (Mathews 1974: 197).

The Big Ten Conference appointed a committee to look into the complaints of Black athletes that found evidence to support the athletes' charges of academic neglect and athletic exploitation. Changes were instituted to improve academic support and counselling for Black athletes, and efforts were made to recruit more Black coaches and other athletic personnel (Wiggins 1989). Big Ten schools, like many other schools during the late sixties and early seventies, hired Black assistant coaches to serve as intermediaries for Black athletes and White head coaches. Problems of discrimination, social isolation and ill treatment by coaches did not disappear, but Black student athletes were more inclined to confront coaches and administrators than they had been in earlier years. These athletes' services were needed now more than ever, and some of their demands had to be met (Wiggins 1989).

Things were not entirely different in Canada, even though it was perceived as a haven from slavery, or as a land of great racial tolerance. For instance, Sam Langford, born near Weymouth, Nova Scotia, in 1886, was considered to be one of the greatest heavyweight boxers of all time. He became famous as the "Boston Tarbaby" after leaving Canada in 1899. Though he may have fought in as many as 659 bouts, he was never allowed to challenge for the title. Black heavyweight titleholder Jack Johnson refused him the opportunity because he reckoned that a fight between two non-Whites would have no box office interest.

In 1913 the Boxing Committee of the Canadian Amateur Athletic Union forbade Blacks to compete in the Canadian championships. This ban lasted into the 1920s (Humber 1985). The attitude of the Canadian Football League (CFL) towards Blacks was no better. In 1946, Lew Hayman, manager of the Montreal Alouettes, stunned his eastern colleagues by signing Black lineman Herb Truwick. Both the Toronto Argonauts and the Ottawa Roughriders threatened to boycott the Montreal team if Truwick played, and they were also upset about Montreal's plan to play on Sundays. According to Hayman,

> What they said was that we just didn't have Sunday games in the league and we simply didn't use Black players. I replied that I couldn't find anything in the rules against either one (quoted in Humber 1985: 521).

And if you talk to the 1991 Canadian Football League rookie of the year, Orville Lee, you will realize that things haven't changed much:

> I saw it up top of the mountain and I saw it in the CFL. The Black athletes are treated differently. Even with something like an injury the racial stereotypes were pervasive. The Black guy was to take a bag of ice and be back playing the next day, while the White guy was given different treatment, which may include ultrasound or whatever. What is that? There is definitely a difference (Interviewed by author 1991).

Even the National Hockey League has had some problems. Commissioner Gary Bettman had to reprimand and then suspend two members of the Washington Capitalists for making demeaning remarks to Black opponents in the heat of a game. There are almost six hundred players on the rosters of the twenty-six National Hockey League, but only a half dozen are Black.

Youth and Sports—My Experience

Sports have always been a very important part of my life. I grew up in a household where sport and its benefits were valued and appreciated. It was part of our upbringing to discuss sport stories at the dinner table on Sunday afternoon. They usually began with stories of great Jamaican athletes such as the Black Streak of Velvet, Herb McKinnley and Donald Quarrie and somehow always ended with my father's recollection of the Oliver Shield or the Manning Cup, schoolboy soccer showdowns in Jamaica in which he and his buddy Gilly were lionized. Interestingly enough, we as a family never tired of hearing those classic tales, secretly hoping we would one day have our own to spin.

As fate would have it, I too now spin a story or two about my sporting days in front of the captive audience of my students. For a long time I was uncertain whether it was the story or the perceived time off from school work that captured their interest. When friends of students who had heard the stories were first asking me to tell them after school, during lunchtime and whenever, this took me by surprise, but I always seized the moment to tell the stories and talk about what sport participation had done for me.

I was born in England of Jamaican parents, Sydney and Enez. They met in Britain while going to school. Like other immigrants, they had left Jamaica hoping to make a better life for themselves and their children. I am the middle child and have an older brother, Everard, and younger sister, Jacqueline. As kids, we were all very active in sports, nurtured by our parents' belief that sports would instill a sense of pride, teach lifelong

Chris Spence as a highschool junior running back, 1979.
(Photo: Centennial High School)

lessons of teamwork and self-discipline, and facilitate physical and emotional development.

Growing up in England, soccer was the sport of choice. I still remember making the weekly trek to the local park to hone our soccer skills under the watchful eye of our father. It became a ritual to come home and talk soccer and dream about someday playing in a organized league. My brother and I quickly became accomplished players, adding soccer skills to our on-again, off-again sibling rivalry. He was always the better athlete, but I the more determined and disciplined.

By the time I was eight we had moved to Canada, as my parents had secured employment in their chosen professions of engineering and nursing. It was an exciting and challenging time for us as a family, but nothing

Chris Spence as a third round draft pick of the BC Lions, 1985.
(Photo: BC Lions Marketing Department)

could have adequately prepared me for the treatment I was about to receive from my peers. It all started with the uniform my parents sent me to school wearing. You see, in England all students wear uniforms to school, so my parents, being new to Canada, assumed the same held true. You can imagine what it was like being the only Black kid in the class, wearing a suit and tie and speaking with a British accent. I became a target for the bullies and the centre of practical jokes, so much so that I practically stopped talking in class out of fear of being ridiculed. I ate lunch by myself everyday and, more often than not, I had to sprint home after school with a couple of goons on my tail, or I would be the last to leave the school, claiming to need extra help, until the coast was clear. I hated going to school. But a soccer game changed all that.

It started out like any ordinary gym period. The teacher picked two individuals to be the captains, Todd and Rick. They went back and forth

Chris Spence, Canadian Football League, Western Conference Semi Final,
BC Place, Vancouver, November 1986.
(Photo: BC Lions Marketing Department)

picking everyone in the class, until only one student was left, and that was me. Neither one of them wanted me on their team, even though they had never seen me play before. At the urging of the teacher, Rick eventually picked me but grabbed me by the scruff of the neck and warned me not to touch the ball or I was dead! Coming from Rick, the class bully, I believed it. The game started and went back and forth. The ball came my way a couple of times and I was tempted to kick it but reminded myself of the threats. The gym teacher, being perceptive, stopped the game wondering why I wasn't participating. To tell her the real reason would have surely meant death. After all, I loved soccer and had been raised playing it. Observing the other players, not even Rick or Todd presented much of a challenge. The next series of events are still a little cloudy, and to this day I don't why I did what I did, but it changed my life.

Decked out in a black suit jacket, white shirt, blue tie, grey pants and black shoes, I was hardly dressed for soccer. Nonetheless, I loosened my tie, took off my jacket and began to play the game of my life. In two minutes I had scored a whopping six goals and earned the adulation and respect of my peers and teachers. Looking back on the whole experience is sometimes painful, but this is a feel-good story. Suddenly I was validated. I mattered in the eyes of my peers. All of a sudden no mountain was too tall to climb. That game brought meaning to my existence, and from that day on a whole new world opened up to me. My confidence would grow in areas outside of sport, academically and socially. And sport continued to open doors in my life that may otherwise have been shut with the same no-trespassing sign that so many others have had to endure.

I am one of the lucky ones, though my parents would not allow me to pay attention to and internalize the limited mass media construction that we Blacks see everyday of ourselves as athletes, entertainers and criminals. I know why so many Black youth choose sport above all else and spend countless hours perfecting their game: validation, the same validation I received from my grade three peers after a soccer game. After all, in what areas does society applaud Black achievements? The answer is sports; and from preschool to university the black male is encouraged to make it in life through sports. I was no different growing up.

I quickly realized that playing on the varsity football team was the surest way to get recognized and treated like a somebody. With all the tradition, envy, adulation and cheerleader interest, my decision to pursue football instead of other sports was easy. Eventually, I earned an athletic scholarship to Simon Fraser University (the only Canadian university to give out scholarships and play exclusively American competition), went on to obtain a degree in criminology and starred as a running back on the football team. Later, I was drafted in the third round by the B.C. Lions of the Canadian Football League.

The lessons learned from my parents and the sporting life are the driving force behind who I am today, as a husband, father, brother, son, friend and educator. They provided me with the necessary ingredients to attain a B.A., B.Ed., M.Ed. and doctorate in Education. And it all started with a soccer game that changed my life.

Sports Participation in High School

A Carnegie Corporation report, "The Role of Sports in Youth Development," found that the involvement of young people in sports produces multiple benefits for them. At their best, sports programs promote responsible behaviours, greater academic success, confidence in one's abilities, an appreciation of personal health and fitness, and strong social bonds with individuals. Teachers attribute these results to the discipline and work ethic that sports require. The Alberta Schools' Athletic Association (ASAA), in conjunction with the Metro Edmonton High School Athletic Association and the Alberta Centre for Well-Being completed a survey of 883 students in November 1997, undertaken to assess the potential impact that high school athletics has on the lives and attitudes of students in Alberta. Findings showed that student athletes are less likely to smoke than non-athletes (30 percent vs. 44 percent), and, if they do smoke, less likely to smoke heavily. The survey findings also indicated student athletes are less likely to report drinking more than once a week in comparison to non-athletic students (9 vs. 20 percent). "The results of this survey suggest that students who participate in school-based sport programs are good citizens and may be even better school citizens than their non-sport peers," says John Paton, executive director of the ASAA. "School athletes demonstrate positive lifestyle behaviours, such as less smoking and less drug use when compared to non-sport students" (National Federation of State High School Associations n.d.).

Theorists have long viewed school sport as an integration mechanism for individual students, for school organizations and for society at large (Coleman 1985). It has been argued (Evans and Davies 1986; Frey 1986) that team sports, especially interscholastic competitions, offer an opportunity for all students—active athletes, cheerleaders and spectators—to congregate and fight for a common goal. These events are viewed as rituals that socialize youth into some of the basic values of life: competition, determination, fair play and achievement.

Howell, Miracle and Rees (1990) found that sport participation in high school was related to educational attainment five years later, but not to the income of those who did not attend college. Later, using the same sample, they reported that some forms of sport participation affected several measures of educational and occupational motivation, such as valuing academic achievement, self-esteem, college plans, occupational plans and positive attitudes towards the high school experience (Rees, Howell and Miracle 1990).

Melnick, Van Fossen and Sabo (1988), using the nationally representative "High School and Beyond" data, found that girls' athletic participation was positively related to extracurricular involvement, school grades, standardized achievement scores, dropout rates, educational aspirations, college attendance, degrees sought and perceived popularity. They also found effects of sport participation on perceived popularity, extracurricular involvement, school grades, standardized achievement scores, dropout rates, educational aspirations, college attendance, degrees sought, and advancement in college for Hispanic boys and girls from urban, suburban and rural areas (Melnick, Sabo and Van Fossen 1992). In a subsequent study, Melnick, Sabo and Van Fossen (1993) reported other differential effects on the educational and occupational attainments of Black, White and Hispanic boys and girls from different areas; sport participation positively affected mostly suburban White male students and, to a lesser degree, White and Hispanic females from rural areas.

Marsh (1993), using the same sample, found that sport participation during the last two years of high school favourably affected fourteen of twenty-two outcomes, including social and academic self-concept, educational aspirations, course work selection, homework, reduced absenteeism and college attendance.

Snyder and Spreitzer (1990) noted six reasons why participation in sport may enhance academic outcomes. Increased participation may lead to:

1. *increased interest in school, including academic pursuits.* The attraction of a college career in sports is often enough motivation for some athletes to strive for good grades.
2. *high academic achievement in order to maintain eligibility to participate in sport.* Student athletes are constantly being made aware of this by their coaches—"No grades, no play."
3. *increased self-concept that generalizes to academic achievement.* One of the benefits of sport participation is the increased self-esteem and self-concept of the participants. It has been suggested that this increased self-concept can spill over to other sectors of the participant's life, namely academics.
4. *increased attention from coaches, teachers and parents.* Coaches, teachers, parents and community have often given the star athlete star treatment, which often includes being graded more leniently, extra help and the like because they are seen

as special or more deserving.

5. *membership in elite groups and an orientation toward academic success.* Student athletes are aware that the road to professional sports goes through the university ranks, which are a recruiting ground for professional teams. The chances of playing professional basketball or football while not playing at the university level are remote.

6. *expectations of participation in university sport.* Student athletes exposed to sports culture are also exposed to the university culture and to expectations that they will move on to participate at the next level.

Ev, an Ontario Academic Credits (OAC) student, who plans to attend university in the fall and play football, is very concerned about his future when his sports career is over:

> I expect to graduate in a couple of weeks and make a decision on what university I will attend. I've been accepted everywhere I have applied, but I'm just not sure if I want to go away or stay home. I know whatever happens for me sportswise, I need an education. My mom tells me that everyday. I realize I can't play forever and I need a good education, because I would like to be a teacher (May 30, 1994).

Robert is a grade nine student who recently completed his first year of high school. He lives with his mother, who emigrated to Canada from Jamaica. She too has emphasized the need for a good education to her son, who discussed the need to stay in school:

> I expect to finish school on time with my diploma and then move on to college or university. That's just the way it has to be. My mom just won't accept anything else. Besides, I want a good job when ball is over. That is why I rate Isiah Thomas: he tore up the court, now he's part owner of the Raptors. You hardly ever see that happening to the brothers. He must be smart to get that (July 11, 1994).

Richard, an OAC student, has high academic expectations:

> I feel I can do anything I want. For me, it is all about putting my mind to it. Right now my focus is track, but academically I'm smart when I want to be and when I'm interested (June 23, 1994).

Pat has plans for university:

> I'll go to university and get my degree; that's a given. And I'll get some job when I'm done. But like a lot of brothers around here, it's ball that is going to give me that chance (July 7, 1994).

All four of these young Black men state their desire for a good education. Sport, for them, is not the totality of their lives, and they acknowledge that their athletic careers will have a limited duration.

Negotiating Identities

A number of studies of the role of athletic participation in the value system of adolescents has replicated research originally conducted by Coleman in 1961, who assigned status to various high school roles by asking students how they would like to be remembered after high school. Male high school students, when asked to choose between being remembered as an athletic star, most brilliant or most popular, selected the role of athletic star most frequently (44 percent). Although this study had predominantly White subjects and would have benefited from a broader, more representative sample, it does have relevance.

Black student athletes closely identify self-esteem and self-confidence with success in sport. And perseverance during training to become a starter in sport may also improve academic pursuits. One informant recognized what sport has done for him:

> I think it really helps my self-esteem. When you feel good in sports, it helps you feel like you can do anything, like school or math, whatever (July 9, 1994).

Another student athlete agreed: ·

> Sports make me feel like I can do anything I want. They teach you cooperation and teamwork. It is also a great pressure releaser. When I do well in a game or practice, I go to class with a very positive attitude. You just feel the confidence everywhere in your life, even if you're talking to a girl (July 17, 1994).

Snyder and Spreitzer (1989) found that preferential treatment of high school athletes (e.g., counselling, leniency in grading, attention from staff and peers) was related to a school's value climate—the more a school values sport, the greater the preferential treatment of its athletes. The salience of sport participation as a source of status, prestige and influence varies from school to school.

As this study suggests, sport participation was a positive experience for the majority of the participants. Thirteen felt that respect (peer approval, admiration by girls, status) was one of the positive aspects associated with sport participation. For example, Cecil stated:

> You get enough respect for playing ball. That's just the way it is. People respect you if you have a game. I don't know anything that carries the same respect as ball (July 5, 1994).

Richard agreed:

> We get a lot of respect. We get a lot more attention than other students because I think they realize we do more. We're not just going to class, we have to practice after school and so forth, and some of us have jobs (June 23, 1994).

Likewise, Damion stated:

> Oh, they treat you real good. I know that is why a lot of brothers play sports. After you play a great game, everybody is bigging you up. It feels real nice walking down the hall after a big game (July 6, 1994).

In keeping with earlier studies, sport participation was found to be an important basis of self-identity and a primary determinant of popularity among peers.

Spreitzer (1994) suggests sports help to "keep kids out of trouble." This assumption is incorporated into the broader belief that "sports build character," that the lessons of sport socialize participants to be good citizens, presumably because, through sport participation, youth are taught conventional values and norms. More specifically, according to this supposition, the training rules of coaches are internalized and function to reduce the deviance of athletes compared to non-athletes. Additionally, even if athletes do not fully internalize conventional expectations, they will not violate the norms because of fear that they will be disciplined by the coach or school officials.

Spreitzer's line of reasoning can easily become classist and racist when used as a justification for implementing programs for Black and underprivileged youth—the underlying message is that society can pay now, or pay the costs later for the detention and counselling of these youth.

The topic of delinquency deterrence has interested sport sociologists for a number of years. For example, one of the earliest studies was conducted by Schafer and Armer (1969), who claimed that sport participation serves as a deterrent to delinquency. Surveying high school students, he found a negative relationship between sport participation and delinquent behaviour.

Informants in my study also mentioned the impact that sports have had on their "staying out of trouble." Savid stated:

> The biggest impact sports have had on me is the people I hang out with. They are almost all athletes and they all want to go on to college and university. The guys I used to hang out with weren't really thinking that way. I think that when you hang with people like that, it rubs off on you. My mom feels a lot better about what I'm doing or want to do with my life (July 29, 1994).

Holland and Andre (1987) reviewed empirical studies of the effects of participation in extracurricular activities, particularly sport, on a wide variety of outcomes. Participation in sport tends to be positively correlated with academic achievement, educational and occupational aspirations, self-concept, popularity and decreased delinquency.

Less delinquency was mentioned to me frequently by teachers and students as a positive result of sport participation. T.J. claimed:

> They have been a saviour for me. Without sports, I don't know what I'd be doing. They have kept me out of trouble and have got me thinking straight about my life (June 3, 1994).

Rudy agreed:

> Every teacher who tries to get me involved in sports has always mentioned that sports can help me as a person. I think they're right. Sports have kept me off the street and out of trouble. And for the most part, sports have kept me in school (June 9, 1994).

Heather, an administrator with twenty-three years of experience, also believes sport participation deters delinquency. She commented on the role of the school in encouraging the sport participation of Black youth:

> The school plays a role. Teachers and administrators tend to think that if you are involved in sports, you won't be involved in other things, which might be related to gangs or drugs (June 1, 1994).

It would be interesting to conduct the same kind of study with White student athletes, to find out if delinquency is a stereotype that teachers hold about Blacks, or whether it is a concern for all student athletes and non-athletes.

In the study for this book, participants placed inordinate emphasis on sport participation. This preoccupation can be attributed to limited social and economic opportunities. Cashmore concludes that "the Black sportsmen sees sport not as a hobby, but as a central life interest, a sphere in which he might find scope and self-expression and a possible avenue out of his mundane, everyday existence" (1982a: 51). Cashmore's finding was supported by my study.

The question that remains is: Does sport participation positively affect the career and academic aspirations of Black male student athletes? The overwhelming response was yes, from both student athletes and teachers and administrators. The teachers and administrators proceeded with caution, however, and almost always referred to the need to balance sport and academics. Olivia, a grade nine science teacher, commented:

> For sure, it is positive, but there has to be the balance of the academics in there. Together they are a terrific combination. One without the other can be limiting, especially if the one is sports (June 11, 1994).

Suzanne, a physical education teacher with four years of teaching experience, agreed. She related the effects of sport participation to events in her brother's life:

> Oh, I think it's positive. There are just so many things you can learn from sport. I see what it has done for my brother. He has a lot of discipline and I think that comes from getting up in the morning to go to hockey practice. He's a real team player and I think that will be very valuable to him in the work place (June 14, 1994).

Student athletes were also vocal about the positive effects of sport participation. For instance, Lou stated:

> I'm only in grade ten, but I honestly don't know if I would have lasted this long without ball. Sometimes it's the only reason I want to get up in the morning (July 29, 1994).

Sport is an important aspect of school culture, and its status in a given school depends on community norms and values, as well as on the relative power of the principal, coaches and teachers. A strong sport culture undoubtedly increases male student participation. The status derived from social, academic or athletic achievement will vary depending on the value placed on these activities in particular schools.

It is evident from this study that teachers need to understand the need of Black male students to excel both on and off the playing field. In fact, all the Black student athletes interviewed are striving to go beyond the limitations and obstacles of their economic background and race.

Anderson et al. (1990) used a three-stage career choice process identified by Ginzberg, Ginzberg and Herma (1951) to address career attainment for Black athletes. It was assumed that the occupational decisions and plans of youth become increasingly realistic as youth gain experience with the opportunity structure and begin to assess their abilities in certain areas more rationally (Ginzberg, Ginzberg and Herma 1951; Picou, Campbell and Campbell 1975).

The first stage of this process is called the "fantasy stage," during which one is unaware of personal capabilities and contingencies associated with occupational achievement. The second stage is the "tentative stage," during which one begins to understand occupation within the context of both personal ability and structural opportunity. The final stage is the "realistic stage," which is characterized by increasingly objective appraisals of career choice.

Experience tells me many athletes become fixated at the fantasy stage and this continues into what should be the realistic stage. Anderson and associates (1990) contend that the tentative stage of career choice can be eliminated by intense socialization for an athletic role during the high school years. As a result, many athletes have little or no basis for making a realistic assessment of all the contingencies associated with becoming a professional athlete.

I never realized how far out of touch some youth were until I heard a thirteen-year-old Black kid talk about his professional basketball aspirations: "Yeah, I'll be in the NBA someday, making Pepsi commercials with Shaq and the boys." This came from someone who did not even play on his middle school team.

There is nothing wrong with having goals; the problem is that, realistically, less than one percent will ever see that goal achieved. What happens to all the rest? Many will spend countless hours on the playground playing the sport they love, helping to make the great ones even greater.

Ginzberg, Ginzberg and Herma (1951) further contend that there are Black/White differences in this pattern. Black athletes were identified as having less academic orientation and more sport orientation. Using a national sample of college basketball players, the authors found that 66 percent of Black Division 1 players expressed an interest in a professional athletic career, compared to only 32 percent of Whites. The authors also found that Black athletes more often desired to forego classes and just play sports than White athletes. This pattern was stronger for Division 1 players. And again, Black athletes were more likely than Whites to have a sport orientation. These authors concluded that Black athletes should receive specific counselling to reduce the negative impact of sport participation on academic achievement.

The centrality of Black student athletes' preoccupations with sport has been well documented. Solomon's two-year ethnographic study (1992) at a Metropolitan Toronto vocational high school documents Black students' preoccupation with sports. This identity formation is encouraged by teachers, coaches, peers and Black role models in the media. The academic needs of these students are compromised, and they turn to sports as a channel for social advancement after realizing that the conventional route through education is not always open.

Almost all informants from my study stated that they spent more time practising and playing their sport than studying. They often cited the need to improve their athletic skills to earn a scholarship and a free education. T.J.:

> I would have to say [I spend] a lot more [time] with sports because that is the way I'm getting out of here. Sports can get me a free education (June 3, 1994).

It appears that many of the student athletes interviewed have bought into the concept of sports as a means to a free education. Marcus, a grade ten student, asked where he spends more time, supports this claim:

> Easily sports . . . just because I want to make it to play at college. I think that is my best chance of getting an education after high school (July 25, 1994).

Rudy:

> More time with sports because that is where I need to work hardest if I'm going to get a scholarship (June 9, 1994).

O.J.:

> I spend more time on sports. Sports are my release. School work is pure tension and boring (May 31, 1994).

James:

> This is our way out to make it big. How many Blacks do you see doing well that aren't in sports? Or sorry, don't forget music. There just aren't that many kicking like Shaq—that guy has everything. I'm not cooperating, I'm dreaming (June 9, 1994).

Mo:

> From what I know and see, this sport is my best opportunity to make it (May 31, 1994).

John:

> It's just a way of getting by. Some teachers try and tell us we can do anything. Let's get real. Can you see me as the Prime Minister? But if I ask you, can you see me in the NBA, everyone is going to say yup (June 1, 1994).

Dawn, a teacher, referred to the emphasis on economics in today's society:

> They see sports as a way out. This society emphasizes money above everything else. It doesn't matter in some peoples' mind how you get the money, as long as you get it. Black kids just don't see education as a vehicle of social mobility. They see sports as something that can get them where they want to go (June 1, 1994).

This view is supported by researchers on Black youth and sport in Britain. Commenting on the socializing impact of schools with teachers as agents, Carrington writes:

> Sports gives them [West Indian pupils] a chance of success. Whereas they're not successful in the classroom, they can show their ability on the sports field (1983:52).

Cashmore's (1982a and 1982b) findings suggest that many teachers perceive Black pupils as having superior physical endowments and skills and rationalize their sporting achievements in naturalistic terms. My research further indicated that some pupils had internalized these stereotypes. For example, one Black youth, when asked to comment on his school's athletic success, remarked:

It's because of the coloured blood. If it wasn't for the coloured blood, our school wouldn't be as good as it is (Cashmore 1982b: 191).

In Britain, as in other societies where race remains a major determinant of life chances, sport continues to provide a small minority of the Black population with a permitted avenue of upward social mobility. Cashmore earlier noted:

> Music and sports are areas in which Blacks have made the most celebrated and acclaimed contribution. Even if the odds are stacked dauntingly against Blacks in most spheres of society, the numbers of Black musicians and sportsmen provide living proof that success can be gained. . . . Black kids, suspicious about their chances of gaining success in regular employment in the system, look to alternative models upon which to base their own role in society (1982a: 70–71).

The majority of the informants from my study agree and believe sports provide an opportunity that does not exist in other sectors of society. Pat explained:

> Today most Black kids feel the only way they can make it anywhere is through sports or entertainment. That is why you see so many Black kids playing basketball—they see it as their future. If you play well enough, you can get a free education. I feel that it is the only way to go to a good school and get a good education. I think it is positive because you can get a free education and make a lot of money. All those pros are our role models (July 7, 1994).

Mo, a grade ten student who hopes to play pro ball one day, supported this claim:

> When you come from the projects, sports is all you know. This is your way out, so you have to be good. I bet most of the pro ball players are from the projects like me and had to work hard to get out. I think it is positive because you get a lot of exposure and you can do a lot of things to help others coming up. If those guys weren't playing pro ball, what would they be doing? (May 31, 1994).

Ev:

> Because Blacks are the best athletes, they dominate all the major sports. To be Black and to be the best is difficult because they are always trying to dog you, and make some White guy like Larry Bird or Gerry Cooney the man (May 30, 1994).

James:

> Sports are our way out. So many Blacks have made it big and they come back and tell all us guys you have to work hard and stay in school. Then a couple of us will make it and we'll say the same thing. Every time we turn on the TV, we will know it's true we can make it to the pros (June 8, 1994).

Therefore, while other communities entertain a variety of ways in which they can advance, Blacks harbour a much more narrowly defined set of possibilities. Wendy, a mathematics teacher, spoke of the perception of limited avenues of social mobility:

> The students react to their environment. If you only have option A and B, then you will strive to achieve A or B. This is what I see with Black youth. I think they have internalized so many of the stereotypes and negative perceptions. Obviously, it is a narrow focus and sports is the focus (June 20, 1994).

Chapter 3

Race and Sport

Winston carries his lunch tray to a table in the far corner of the cafeteria, tucked away near the exit, and takes a seat next to Jammal and Derek. The three Black students sit there in the corner, eating, playing dominoes and carrying on a conversation, oblivious to the other students in the cafeteria. In a half hour or so, they leave and are replaced by a new group of diners. The names will change but the scene will stay the same: Black students at their tables and non-Blacks at theirs. Such is the scene in many high schools, and it was not that different in sports.

In 1985, when I first arrived in the Canadian Football League, players typically segregated themselves off the playing field. On the airplane, Blacks sat with Blacks, and Whites sat with Whites. On away trips, Blacks dressed one way and Whites another. After the game, Blacks went their way, usually to a club, and Whites went their way. And unless a coach designated interracial roommates, voluntary segregation was the rule there as well.

Racism in sports is not different from racism everywhere. People are afraid of what they don't know. Many White football players hate rap music, which some Black players take pleasure in playing loud in the dressing room before and after practice. The same can be said of Blacks and their hate of rock 'n roll. Many Blacks have been victims of racism and many Whites come from backgrounds where they were unaccustomed to interacting with Blacks. It's hard to all of a sudden drop your defences just because the guy next to you is wearing the same uniform.

One thing cannot be denied in any discussion of sport these days. Blacks do represent the dominant force in terms of numbers and starting positions. The emergence of White starters, such as Keith Van Horn of the New Jersey Nets, becomes a huge story, as writers seek out the next Larry Bird. In fact, this has become so much of an issue that Spartanburg Methodist College, a junior college in South Carolina, recently instituted a quota system to bring more White players into its basketball program. The school, which is 73 percent White, had an all-Black basketball team. The goal was to obtain a 60-40 Black-White quota on the team. The coaches were stunned, and eventually fired for refusing to comply with the quota policy.

Much has also been made of the fact that the New York Giants' Jason

Sehorn is the only White starter in the entire National Football League at cornerback, a position in which speed, reaction time and athleticism are crucial.

Make no mistake about it, race continues to be an issue in sport. Of all the values in North American culture, perhaps none is more romanticized than the belief that sport is the great equalizer—and it is deemed that way because the bottom line is winning, and putting a winning team on the field.

Issues of race continue to come to the forefront of sports. Latrell Sprewell, a Black basketball player, attacks his White coach. *Sports Illustrated* and ESPN, sports communication giants, produce special reports that chronicle the domination of sports by Black athletes. The cover of a special edition of *Sports Illustrated* asks the burning question: "What Happened to the White Athlete?" A Massachusetts high school principal notices a trend at his high school: many White students begin to wear ND (Notre Dame) caps, while Black students begin to wear UNLV (University of Nevada, Las Vegas) ones. The principal discovers a disturbing reason for this. Some of the White students claim to be wearing the ND cap to send a hate message—"Niggers Die." Black students reacted with the UNLV caps—"Us Niggers Love Violence." Fuzzy Zoeller jokes that he hopes Tiger Woods won't order fried chicken and collard greens for his Masters' dinner and almost immediately loses his endorsement deal. Marge Schott, owner of the Cincinnati Reds, referred to her Black players by a well-known racial slur, defended Hitler and was suspended from baseball. Jack Nicklaus opined that the physical design of Blacks prevented them from excelling at golf (Lopchick 1996).

The images frequently found in popular media assist in institutionalizing and internalizing stereotypes about Black athletes. For example, Nolan Richardson, a Black basketball coach at the University of Arkansas, was talking about the strengths of his conference. He referred to the athleticism of many of the players and suggested that it is no surprise given that many of them are from the South. A reporter asked what the South had to do with athletic ability. "Where did the slave ships stop?" the coach asked, "Where did they stop? In the South, you have a tremendous amount of Black kids who are athletically inclined." Nate Newton of the Dallas Cowboys sounded a lot like Jimmy the Greek when he explained that more good football players come from Florida because they are descendants of Africans bred during slavery. CBS Sports analyst Billy Packer was criticized for his reference to Allan Iverson—a Black basketball star at Georgetown University and now with the Philadelphia 76ers—as "a tough monkey." Packer appeared not to recognize the sensitivity of the remark and expressed surprise at the reaction to it. For Blacks, the monkey slur is particularly harmful because of centuries-old efforts to dehumanize Blacks by associating them genetically with primates (Lapchick 1996).

A stereotype is "a largely false belief or set of beliefs concerning the characteristics of the members of a racial or ethnic group" (McLemore 1991: 137). It is a distorted picture of a category of people that the outgroup, and sometimes even the in-group, members accept as part of cultural or racial heritage. Furthermore, by ignoring or explaining away contradictory evidence, people reinforce stereotypes; overgeneralizations are treated as if they are true (Davis 1978). Stereotypes resist change, although contemporary events can alter or weaken beliefs. For much of their history, people of African descent were believed to be superstitious, lazy, happy-go-lucky and ignorant (McLemore 1991). Secondary structural assimilation—the movement of Blacks into previously segregated schools, occupations and other institutions—has been accompanied by a diminution of the salience of these stereotypes in many areas of life. However, major American and Canadian sports, in spite of their inclusion of Blacks in player positions, have retained many racial stereotypes.

Almost all of my informants expressed anger at the perceived lack of respect given to them by their teachers, and frequently articulated race as the reason for teachers and administrators nurturing Black students' interest in sports. Hansen, an OAC student who aspires to work in the field of computers one day, stated:

> They try to push us into [sports]. They influence us to go into sports to take us away from the academic part. I guess they think that is all we're good for. They don't give us respect for our minds. They just want us to represent the school on the playing field (June 4, 1994).

Many other informants agreed. Mo:

> As far back as I remember to elementary school they were encouraging me to join the track team. They do it because some are racist, they don't think we have any intelligence (May 31, 1994).

O.J.:

> I feel that a lot of teachers/coaches steer the Black kids away from the academics and into athletics. If they were to steer us into academics, we would control that as well. If I miss a class, no one cares; but if I miss a practice or game and can't represent the school, then it's trouble (May 31, 1994).

Quinn:

> Yeah they do. . . . I know why: they think that is all we can do. When they see Black, they see dealers and athletes (July 15, 1994).

Nigel:

> They ask you to come out for teams, then try to make you feel like you're a sellout if you don't come out. Certain teachers around here who we all know are racist don't say a word to us until it is ball season. They want to win and know they need us (May 31, 1994).

Wiggins states:

> Blacks are thought to possess natural athletic ability in speed, quickness, and jumping ability; traits that many coaches believe cannot be taught—you are either born with these qualities or you do without them. That they excel in sport, then, has little to do with their work ethic or their intellect, according to this perspective. This view allows Blacks to be outstanding athletes without negating the belief that they are lazy and ignorant; in fact, it reinforces the belief in their indolence and incognizance. This is what I think some sports fans (and fans of Black athletes) had in mind when they stated their admiration for the athletic gift bestowed on Black athletes and followed that by asking, "Without inborn talent, where would the black athlete be? What do you think his fate would be if he had to work as hard as the white athlete?" (1989: 61–62).

Whites, on the other hand, are believed to excel at sport because they possess traits that are valued both in and especially out of sport: intelligence, industriousness and other unspecified intangibles (Harris 1990). Athletic ability is a limiting but not deciding factor in White sport participation. According to this view, they rely on other traits to overcome their mediocre endowment.

An article entitled, "The Best in College Hoops," which appeared in *Sport* magazine in January 1991, illustrates this last point. In describing the top four point guards in college basketball, the article made the following assessments:

> **(1) Kenny Anderson (Georgia Tech)**—Kenny has superb in-

stincts, unbelievable quickness, and he's also amazingly mature for his age. . . . But . . . he often shoots when he should pass, a serious indictment for a point guard.

(2) **Bobby Hurley (Duke)**—So what's the deal here? Hurley's a team genius, the type of kid coaches love to love. . . . From a team point of view—and what other point of view is there for a point guard?—this perceptive penetrator does every bit as much for the Blue Devils as Anderson does for Tech.

(3) **Chris Corchiani (North Carolina State)**—If he gets the ball on the move, he's almost impossible to stabilize. Still, many experts question CC Rider's quickness and outside shot. Legitimate queries. But with a guy like Chris, his intangibles will always outweigh his ability.

(4) **Lee Mayberry (Arkansas)**—"Mayberry's a brilliant athlete and a great passer, but not a true point guard. He just doesn't think like one," says Hamilton. "More often than not, I disagree with his decision-making" (Kertes 1991: 70).

Anderson and Mayberry are Black. The writer gives them credit for their physical abilities but has reservations about their mental abilities. The White players—Hurley and Corchiani—are described as lacking the physical skills of Anderson and Mayberry, but they make up for it with cognitive abilities and "intangibles." Thus, although the writer appears to be honouring Anderson and Mayberry by including them in this exclusive group, he is, in fact, reproducing one of the most pervasive stereotypes of Blacks: they have the tools, but their intellects are questionable. The real praise is reserved for the White players, because they have managed to prevail despite what the writer perceives to be their modest athletic endowment (Harris 1990).

The persistence of stacking in college football is a product of the same stereotype. (Stacking is the practice of assigning individuals to sport positions on the basis of race or ethnicity.) Blacks are still primarily relegated to positions that are said to require speed, quickness and jumping ability. The rare player, Black or White, who occupies a position that deviates from the expectations for members of his group finds that his abilities are redefined in ways that are consistent with the race-linked stereotypes. To quote Tom Waddle, a White wide receiver for the Chicago Bears:

When you don't fit into the computer on things like size, speed and vertical jump, you are basically a reject. You are a possession receiver. A possession receiver is a polite term for slow (Kertes 1991: 3).

"Possession receiver" is a term used almost exclusively for White receivers.

Even the presence of Blacks in positions that have been traditionally reserved for Whites tends to support rather than refute stereotypes about athletic ability. Many Black college quarterbacks are required to gain significant yards by running the ball. They often accumulate as many yards as, if not more than, the halfbacks or tailbacks on their teams. In other cases, when they exhibit proficiency as passers, they still find it difficult for coaches and professional scouts to take their accomplishment seriously (Wiggins 1989). For example, no NFL team started a Black at quarterback until the 1970s, and the first Black head coach didn't arrive until 1989. The CFL, however, has provided many Blacks the opportunity to compete at quarterback, and was a training ground for Warren Moon, who went on to NFL stardom.

Today, an ill-informed and substantially racist argument is still prevalently made that Blacks are biogenetically different, distinct and uniquely endowed with some presumed gene-based, race-linked capacity for sports achievement. Sport participation is therefore perceived as a natural and immutable Black calling (Edwards 1992).

Throughout my study, issues of race were raised by the informants. One question provided them with an opportunity to respond to a racist statement—"The perfect athlete has the Black body and the White mind"— and they did so with passion and anger. Pat took exception to the statement and pointed his finger at the media and racism:

> We're just not known for our brains. The media tries to hide it. Look what they do with Cito Gaston—just because he is Black. He wins two back-to-back World Series and you never see him on television or in the papers. Nobody rates Cito as a smart coach. This is really racist. White people do that because they think we don't read too much (July 7, 1994).

Other informants were just plain angry and did not hold back their disapproval. Kirk:

> That is just a stereotype—but that really sucks. We are smart too. That really pisses me off, and that is probably what a lot of those teachers think as well (June 1, 1994).

Quinn:

> What a bullshit statement! Blacks can do anything. If we were pushed in that direction, we would control it as well (July 15, 1994).

James:

> Here we go again. I can't even respond to that statement. It is just plain ignorant. It must have been a White person who said that (June 8, 1994).

O.J.:

> See what I mean. Black people get no respect. I heard no shit like that before. That's why there are no Black quarterbacks. Same old story. I don't accept that at all. The best college quarterbacks are Black; they just don't give them a chance. That really pisses me off (May 31, 1994).

Martin Kane, a senior editor with *Sports Illustrated*, ignited the age-old debate over Black superiority by claiming, in an article titled "An Assessment of Black is Best," that "there is an increasing body of scientific opinion which suggests that physical differences in the races might well have enhanced the athletic potential of the Negro in certain sports." Kane (1971) argued that the dominance of Black athletes in sport was the result of racially linked psychological, historical and physiological factors. The outstanding performances of Black athletes, in other words, arose from characteristics indigenous to the Black population. Some individuals believe that the superior body build of the Black athlete was contrived, either directly or indirectly, by Whites. They argue that only the fittest and healthiest of Blacks survived the trip from Africa in the overcrowded, disease-ridden slave ships, and that today's Black athletes are the descendants of those survivors. This belief has been labelled "The Survival of the Fittest Theory" (Sailes 1990). Also, since most Black communities have been underfunded, with no tennis courts or swimming pools, Black kids grow up playing low-cost sports such as basketball and football. The competition on these inner city courts and makeshift fields is where their skill levels are raised to new heights.

My own success in sport definitely has to be attributed to effort. I had to work harder than everyone else and took great pride in that. Although my father was a very capable sportsman in his day, my mother was not actively involved in sports, nor was she interested. Most of us have abilities we've never used because no one has encouraged us to develop them. High jumpers often achieve more than they thought they could, simply because their coaches keep raising the bar.

Although some physical differences are apparent between Black and White populations, it remains to be demonstrated that anatomical and/or physiological differences between Black and White athletes contribute significantly to the dominance of either in sports competition (Coakley 1990; Davis 1990; Eitzen and Sage 1989). Steele (1990) argues that one race-oriented component of White superiority and Black inferiority is intelligence. Support for the physical superiority myth indirectly contributes to the belief that the Black athlete is mentally and intellectually inferior to the White athlete (Davis 1990; Hoose 1989). Assumptions about the "dumb jock" are linked to racial stereotypes. This racist attitude leads to the discriminatory practice of channelling Blacks away from the central leadership and decision-making positions in college and professional sport (Coakley 1990; Eitzen and Sage 1989; Leonard 1988). For example, Al Camparis, former Los Angeles Dodgers general manager, exposed racial stereotyping in sport when he made the assertion on national television that Blacks may not have the "necessities" to be managers in professional baseball (Hoose 1989). About 70 percent of Black players in Major League Baseball play in the outfield (Lapchick 1996). This practice of limiting Black players' roles is prevalent among college and professional baseball and football teams (Schneider and Eitzen 1986).

Here are areas where disparities remain:

Ownership of teams: No Black owners exist; Isiah Thomas's stint as a minority owner of the Toronto Raptors is history.

Top front-office jobs: The NBA has the best record in this category, with Blacks in 28 percent of the general manager or player personnel directors jobs, according to a 1996 report by Northeastern University's Center for the Study of Sport in Society. There are only four Blacks in those positions in the NFL and one in Major League Baseball, where Bob Watson of the World Series champion New York Yankees is the only Black general manager.

Coaches and managers: The NBA again has the best record in the Northeastern report (Lapchick 1996), with 20 percent of the head coaching and 41 percent of the assistant coaching positions occupied by Blacks. In baseball and football, about one in ten head coaches and one in five assistants are Black. The NFL came under criticism by a group of Black assistants after eleven new head coaches were hired after the 1996 season, but none of them was Black. Brody (1993) found the situation in college sports no better. He found that although 60 percent of college basketball players were Black, only 19 percent of the managers and coaches were; and although 40 percent of college football players were Black, Blacks filled only three percent of the manager and coach positions. In fact, Brody reports that only nine colleges have ever employed a Black head football coach and only three schools have Black athletic directors. The Rainbow Coalition for Fairness in Athletics has begun to rate NCAA Division 1 schools for several factors, including the number of Black athletes, graduation rates for Blacks and the number of Blacks in coaching and administrative positions. In 1990, at predominantly White Division 1 schools, there were only 47 Black head coaches among the 1,165 head coaches in football, men's and women's basketball, track and baseball—only 4 percent of the positions (Lapchick 1991). Casual observation of Canadian university and college coaching staffs reveals a discouragingly similar pattern.

On-field positions: Black players now can be found almost anywhere on the field in the big three sports. But certain "thinking" positions, such as quarterback in football and infielder in baseball, remain dominated by Whites, while more "athletic" positions, such as running back and out-fielder, are where Blacks are stacked.

Traditionally White sports: For various geographic, economic and other reasons, sports such as ice hockey, golf, tennis, auto racing, lacrosse, skiing and volleyball are rarely played on a high level by Blacks. But as Tiger Woods has shown, the impact can be dramatic when someone does break through.

Sports media: Newspapers and broadcast companies have been more aggressive in recent years in hiring and promoting Black commentators, but four of every five radio and television announcers are White. That means the images of sports and Black athletes continue to be shaped largely by White men. In fact, 90 percent of America's 1,600 daily news-papers do not have a single Black writer on their staffs.

Sports merchandise companies: Georgetown coach John Thompson sits on the board of directors for Nike, but with the unusual power amassed by shoe companies in the past decade, and the money they have amassed from Black youth, there have been calls for more Black partici-pation.

Salaries: The salaries of professional athletes are unfairly distributed by race when performance is controlled. For example, Koch and Vanderhill (1988) examined the 1984–85 salary structure of NBA professional basket-ball and found that equal pay for equal work does not exist. They found that Blacks would be paid $17,832 more per year if they were White and had similar performance statistics.

Sadly, too few people notice that Black sporting success can be in part explained by what Blacks have above the neck. Unfortunately, books like *The Bell Curve* (Murray and Hernstein 1996), which contends that Asians and Whites tend to be smarter than Blacks, continue to prevail. How can just one number represent all the many kinds of mental talents? Let us not forget the IQ test was invented by a Frenchman, so it is not surprising it is good at gauging what the French value most: impersonal reasoning in a formal setting.

A poll commissioned and reported by William Johnson (1991) in *Sports Illustrated* found that a large percentage of non-White professional athletes felt that White players were given preferential treatment by teams. Over 70 percent of Black athletes surveyed believed that non-Whites had to be more talented than Whites to make a team's roster, and almost 50 percent thought that owners had racial quotas. Professional athletes are glaring exceptions to the norm, yet mainstream society sees their successes and is able to sleep at night, thinking that equality is a reality.

Society is still haunted by the ghosts of slavery. The racial discrimination and oppressed urban conditions which grew out of slavery still linger on, hindering Blacks from socio-economic mobility.

Black college athletes are being used to bring recognition and wealth to their schools. Many members of the public believe that if these Blacks give their athletic ability to a university for four years, then the school is expected to give them the opportunity to receive an education. Coaches and schools are making a fortune off of these athletes, but too many are leaving college without a meaningful education. For this reason, I have been skeptical of tracking graduation rates, because those numbers reveal only how many athletes received a degree, not how many received an education.

College and professional sports resemble modern "plantations" where White owners and administrators treat their athletes like property.

Sport and the Socialization of Black Children

Socialization can be defined as the process by which we learn the practices of a given social group so we can function within it (Elkin and Handel 1989). Most complex modern societies contain a variety of ethnic groups, which are the primary sites of socialization. Elkin and Handel (1989) point out that children are not initially socialized into the culture as a whole; rather they are socialized into a particular ethnic culture. As a result, children may not initially learn the ways of the larger society but will adopt the more specific ways of their own particular societal segment. Elkin and Handel define culture as:

> A way of life developed by a people in adaptation to the physical and social circumstances in which they find themselves. It tends to be passed on from generation to generation, but it changes as circumstances change. It includes some elements that are highly valued by the people themselves and other elements that are accepted as necessary or "realistic" adaptations but are not especially valued (1989: 81).

For a child, the family provides the first significant definition of what it means to be human. Most parents socialize their children to become self-sufficient, competent adults as defined by the society or sub-society in which they live (Peters 1981). Certain values and norms are perceived as necessary adaptations to be passed on from generation to generation. For example, Black families encourage the development of the skills, abilities and behaviours necessary for youth to survive as competent adults in a racially oppressive society (Willie 1976).

In the context of sport, socialization is more than just learning rules, wearing uniforms, establishing rituals or adopting a competitive ideology. These are just one part of the symbolic meaning of sport, and hence only one dimension of the sport socialization process. Socialization also includes a symbolic reproduction of the larger political, economic and cultural ideology (Goodman 1985).

Sport participation is very much a part of male socialization. And sport has taken on particular significance in Black neighbourhoods. Many less-affluent Black males place tremendous emphasis on successful participation in organized sport. Many Black youth view sport as their only opportunity for social and material success, especially when doors to other opportunities appear to be closed. This is illustrated by the overrepresentation of Blacks in particular sports and their under-representation in other segments of society. As we have seen, Black males constitute 80 percent of the athletes in professional basketball, 60 percent in professional football and 20 percent in professional baseball. However, less than two percent of Black males are doctors, lawyers, architects, college professors or business executives (Sailes 1990).

A cultural norm has developed among lower-income Blacks that, for boys, the rite of passage to manhood is through sport. This norm places importance on the values that are apparent in an athlete's attitude, behaviour and sport participation.

The Center for the Study of Sport and Society at Northeastern University revealed that a Black family is seven times more likely to push a male child into sport than a White family, and the National Collegiate Organization (NCO) revealed that 50 percent of Black athletes playing Division 1 football and basketball come from impoverished backgrounds. Even more frightening is the statistical data from the National Urban League which reveals more Black males are in prison than are attending colleges (Sailes 1990).

These findings suggest that specific institutional factors and cultural norms have an impact on the socialization of inner city Black males. If sports are indeed more highly emphasized within the Black subculture, this fact may help to explain the willingness of Blacks to participate in various types of sport contests even when discriminatory practices are encountered.

Edwards (1983) suggests four reasons why sports tend to be more salient in the Black subculture: (1) Black males spend a greater amount of time honing their athletic skills while believing they will become professional athletes, (2) there is a dearth of highly visible Black role models in fields other than sports and entertainment, (3) the Black family and community tend to overreward achievement in athletics relative to other forms of achievement and (4) Black males are more likely to see sport participation as a way of proving their manhood.

The perception that sport offers Blacks unique socioeconomic and career advancement opportunities has prompted Black parents to be four times more likely that White parents to view their children's participation in sport not as mere recreation but as a start down the road to a professional sports career. Similarly, Black parents are more likely than White parents to see their children's sport participation as a potential economic mobility vehicle for the entire family (Edwards 1992).

This exaggerated emphasis on athletic achievement among the Black community is further intensified by the disproportionate coverage given Black athletes and their accomplishments, rewards and lifestyles by the print and broadcast media. Particularly in depressed areas, Black celebrity athletes, though far removed, are often the principal male role models for starry-eyed young men dreaming of big money and success in professional sports.

Teacher and administrator informants agreed that the media plays a significant role in portraying Black athletes. Commercials and sporting events highlight the successful Black athlete. Queen, an educational administrator, urged the Black community to take control of the media:

> We need to take control of the media and reject the things they show us in stereotyped roles. We have to reject watching shows like "Martin" that continually show us in these demeaning roles. We, as a Black community, need to call into TV stations and say we object to this or that. We just don't do that enough. I heard a phone-in radio show that spoke about the shooting of a police officer. It was Christie Blatchford. She said that the accused, who was from Jamaica, was from a matriarchal society in which Black men demonstrate no responsibility. Now, you tell me, what is a Black male who is listening to this supposed to think? I don't see this in my family. My mother and father have been married for fifty years; I have been married for twenty-seven; my sister, the same. Anyone listening to that would probably believe it, but how many of us will call in and say we object? We need to take charge (June 27, 1994).

Susane, a dramatic arts and English teacher, spoke about the messages aimed at Black youth through the media and society:

> A lot of Black kids would be interested in sports with or without the school. So where does that come from? I'll tell you—it comes from the media and it comes from society. Media has a strong impact on youth. The message for Black youth is to be an entertainer or athlete. Those messages come out loud and clear to me. Teachers see the same thing the kids see. Although we are expected to be more critical of what we view, teachers are also influenced by what they see and hear (June 21, 1994).

Ed, a physical education teacher, agreed:

> Oh yes, [the media play] a huge role. Sports have become a way of raising self-esteem in Black kids and a way of showing money and success. It only makes sense that this is the way that sports is viewed. After, Blacks have succeeded at sports, so it perpetuates itself. The problem is compounded when Blacks don't see the successes in other areas. My biggest fear right now as an educator is the introduction of the Toronto Raptors [Toronto's NBA team]; it's now a step closer to all those youth out there who are dreaming of a professional sports career (August 15, 1994).

For too many of these youngsters, pursuit of athletic glory and riches seems the only route out of poverty. Failure to achieve that dream has, more often than not, left the vast majority of them not only disillusioned but without the fundamental skills to succeed in another walk of life (Edwards 1992).

There are compelling reasons to believe that television's socializing effects may be greater for Black children. Anderson and Williams (1983) cite a Neilson television index indicating that Black families spend significantly more time watching television than White families. Anderson and Williams believe the reasons for this discrepancy are that Black families often have fewer resources, are less mobile and have fewer entertainment alternatives. And, in many cases, television is employed as an inexpensive babysitter or a third parent for the Black child (Anderson and Williams 1983). This excessive television exposure can have a powerful influence on Black youth.

Casual observation of the three most often televised sports—baseball, basketball and football—show a drastic overrepresentation of Blacks. Thus, sport on television provides a pertinent illustration of how Blacks are characterized by the media. Because Black athletes are considered role models for Black youth, how these athletes are portrayed is particularly important. Sportscasters often portray Black athletes as "natural and gifted athletes," whereas White athletes are characterized as "intelligent and hard working" (Wiggins 1989). This discrepancy sends an obvious message and may influence the identity formation of Blacks, partially shaping the child's self-concept. This self-concept may then be integrated into a network of ideas about what abilities Blacks have, what their preferences are and what they can expect to achieve in life. The stereotype of the natural athlete can thus prompt Black youth to focus on particular sport activities.

Environment and Sport Participation

Many apparent racial differences stem from circumstances of environment. People work harder on what they find rewarding and walk away from what they find frustrating in their environment.

Several sociologists have theories about the environmental factors that influence Blacks to participate in sport. Edwards (1971) contends that as long as sport provides the only visible, high status, occupational role model for masses of Black youth, Blacks will continue to be overrepresented in sport activities. Phillips (1976) maintains that Black athletes will excel most in sports where they have access to the best facilities, coaching and competition.

Carlston (1983) offers an environmental explanation for racial differences in basketball performance, insisting that these differences are a product of the circumstances under which the racial groups learn to play. Inner-city basketball courts are often crowded with large numbers of players competing for playing time. The inner-city player has to learn to dribble, drive and shoot successfully, or his time on the court will be limited. Because the winners remain on the court, the most skilled players play more and get more practice. This is in contrast to the non-inner-city game in which the central problem is player scarcity. The non-inner-city player develops playing skills relatively free from the pressure of competition, in an environment vastly different from that of the actual game.

As Blacks are often the major occupants of the inner city, it is easy to see why Black athletes excel in the game of basketball. Black youth gain experience in a special brand of basketball, they are influenced by the profusion of outstanding sport role models and they ultimately incorporate the distinctive style of play of these role models into their own movements. Even though this playing style arises out of the inner city, it is practised by other groups of Blacks. Non-city Black youth sometimes identify with their popular and successful city-dwelling counterparts and may adopt and duplicate these distinct movement patterns and styles. Although individuals can develop a positive athletic self-concept from many different sources, an immediate social environment in which athletic skills are valued can provide youngsters with opportunities to observe skilled play and receive direct and indirect feedback about their performances (Harrison 1995).

The Black Male and Sport

One of the most actively discussed issues has been the declining social, economic and educational status of young Black males in our society. This group's unemployment statistics, homicide rates, overwhelming disproportionate representation in the criminal justice system and last-place ranking on many measures of educational performance and attainment have caused many to view their futures as hopeless.

Since the Moynihan Report (Moynihan 1965), increased attention has been paid to the "absent father" in the Black family. This report found that one of the factors which had directly led to the "deterioration" of the Black family was the high proportion of Black families headed by females (Pinkney 1987; Staples 1986). The report blames Blacks rather than society and fails to recognize that racism perpetuates unequal opportunities and the overrepresentation of Blacks among the poor; it also masks the relationship between poverty and family stability regardless of race. The Moynihan Report is problematic, but it did raise a very pressing issue in the Black community, one that was articulated by student athlete participants.

The absent father was noticeable at the NBA draft in 1995, when research revealed that twenty-three of the top thirty NBA players grew up without their biological fathers, who had left them as tots or adolescents (Clarkson 1995). Shaquille O'Neal, of Los Angeles Lakers fame and a part-time rapper, revealed some of his feelings for the father who abandoned him in his rap song "Biological Didn't Bother."

Sports researcher Varda Burstyn believes "the missing father is one of the key motivators for elite athletes, who try to fill the parental void by reaching for the top of the sports world, which to them can represent a false view of masculinity" (in Clarkson 1995: F5). Like the informants in my study, many suggest that players often use basketball to prove to others that they can be successful, even though they come from the inner city without a father (Clarkson 1995).

Karenga (1980), however, argues that the major problem in the Black community is a lack of a cultural identity. He contends that the media's influence on Blacks, particularly Black males, is maximized in the absence of a strong cultural base and identity. Karenga also maintains that Blacks possess a popular rather than national culture. Popular culture is defined as the "societal perceptions and stereotypes of your group," whereas

67

national culture is more of a self-definition. He states that popular culture is "the unconscious, fluid reaction to everyday life and environment. In other words, it is a social thought and practice defined and limited by its unconsciousness, fluidity and reactiveness." National culture, by contrast, is "the self-conscious, collective thought and practice through which a people creates itself, celebrates itself and introduces itself to history and humanity" (Karenga 1980: 18).

Karenga (1980: 19–20) lists the negative elements of popular culture:

1. high level of reactiveness rather than pro-activeness,
2. high level of hustler values which permeate Black popular culture (e.g., emphasis on quick money at any cost, heavy sex, conning),
3. high level of simple survival orientation (e.g., cockroach existence, just getting by, making it and nothing more),
4. high level of present time orientation (engendered by the vulnerability of an oppressed people and their uncertainty about the future and fear of not being around to enjoy things beyond the immediate),
5. overemphasis on fun and games (which has gone so far that athletics and entertainment have become our most well-known activities as a people) and
6. high level of myth-orientation and grandiose dreams, often shunning the hard work of development and building for religious and social escapism and dreaming.

Similarly, Gaston states:

> The adult Black male frequently finds himself on a fantasy island lacking the skills necessary to propel himself into the flow of the mainstream. I believe that this isolation from the mainstream deprives or severely restricts the Black male's ability to develop the self-concept and the economic potential necessary to develop and nourish a long-range dyadic relationship with the Black woman (1986: 371).

Several researchers have commented on the cultural image of the Black male. Lombardo (1978: 60) notes two distinct stereotypes that have emerged regarding Black males. Known as the "Brute" and the "Sambo" stereotypes, they were developed by Whites to maintain a superior position in society, denigrating Black males and thus keeping them subordinate. The Brute stereotype characterizes the Black male as primitive, temperamental, overreactive, uncontrollable, violent and sexually powerful, whereas the more popular Sambo stereotype depicts him as benign, childish, immature, exuberant, uninhibited, lazy, comical, impulsive, fun-loving, good-humoured, inferior and lovable.

Marble (1986) presents a similar position by suggesting that the essential tragedy of being Black and male is the inability of Black men to define themselves apart from the stereotypes that the larger society imposes on them; he contends that these stereotypes are perpetuated through various institutional means and permeate the entire culture. Mable argues that the historical cultural image of the Black male is conditioned by these basic beliefs:

> Black men were only a step above animals—possessing awesome physical power, but lacking in intellectual ability. As such, their proper role in White society was as labourers, and not as the managers of labour. Second, the Black male represented a potential political threat to the entire system of slavery. And third, the Black male symbolized a lusty sexual potency which threatened White women (1986: 65).

These beliefs not only inform the larger cultural image of the Black male but also influence how the Black male develops his definition of self.

Positive and Negative Sides of Sport Participation

Students can learn many positive values from participating in high school sports. Many of these values cannot be derived from any other part of school life. Being selected for a sports team is a recognition of skill and is associated with social rewards which help to develop a more positive self-concept. The higher social status of male high school athletes (Coleman 1961), together with physical skill itself, can feed the ego and enhance self-esteem (Snyder and Spreitzer 1990).

Participation in sports teams requires adjustment to rigid rules, regulations and practice times, as well as the coach's authority. Enduring long hours of practice, while delaying the fulfilment of other physical and social needs, teaches the rewards associated with compliance, possibly making it easier to accept other school rules and formal authority. Being on a school team also means being recognized by the system as a "good citizen" who participates in community life beyond basic requirements. This may, in turn, create deeper commitment on the part of the student not only to the school's rules but also to its basic values and to academic work. Conforming to school rules and values may result in more disciplined behaviour and higher grades. Higher grades can thus reflect a self-discipline and willingness to put forth effort learned through sport training or teacher inclination to befriend these students (Snyder and Spreitzer 1990).

Positive effects of sport participation on the educational aspirations of male student athletes may be attributed to their plans to use their athletic prowess as "human capital" to gain access to university (Snyder and Spreitzer 1990), their increased social status or their improved self-concept and discipline. Whatever the explanation, this study found that participation in high school competitive sports provides positive experiences that enhance Black student athletes' adjustment to school rules, school work and the basic values of an achievement-oriented society.

However, we still need to address the negative aspects of sport participation. We live in a society where athletes have gotten away with things just because they're athletes. Sharon Stoll, the director of the Center of Ethics at the University of Idaho, has seen it firsthand. She looked at about 25,000 athletes—Division 1 to Division 111, high school athletes, Olympic athletes, and NAIA athletes—and found that they are highly affected by their competitive environment. Their cognitive moral development is lower than what it should be, and significantly lower than that of the general population. Stoll's conclusions are based on volumes of data, many of which measure an athlete's honesty, sense of justice and respect for other people.

Further, a growing body of research suggests that athletic culture breeds problems. Violence against women is widespread and perpetuated overwhelmingly by males. There is something deeply problematic about the way our culture is training boys and men to behave. Male athletes can help effect change, not just within the sport subculture but also in the larger culture, which often looks to them as examples of masculine success.

One of the biggest problems with high school sport is the overemphasis on winning, which occurs when administrators, teachers, parents and the community expect and, in some cases, demand success. This pressure often results in year-round training programs, greater stress for students and less time for academic pursuits. "Friday Night Lights: A Town, a Team and a Dream" is a sobering real-life account of misplaced educational priorities, subtle and not so subtle forms of racism, and the pressures that a football coach and his team feel when much of the pride within their small community comes vicariously through the sustained success of the high school football team. This high school's obsession with sports is not unique. Many other schools have also exploited students and programs, bent or broken the rules and chosen to overlook unethical behaviour to ensure a winning team. In the best interests of athletic programs and the youth they serve, school teachers and administrators must recognize these sorts of problems in their schools and take appropriate steps to correct them.

Participants in this study made it clear that public high schools hunger for victories. The hunger to win at all costs is established at higher levels of play and filters down to the high school. In college ball, the goal is no longer for athletes to test and strengthen their bodies, learn about teamwork and have a good time; all that matters is winning, moving up in the national rankings and grabbing a bigger share of the TV dollar that comes with appearances in the NCAA's game of the week. To achieve these aims, schools and coaches not only bend and break the National College Athletic Association rules, but they also violate the intellectual integrity and principles of the U.S. university system (Purdy, Eitzen and Hufnagel 1982).

The recruitment of superathletes is so critical to a winning program that coaches have offered illegal monetary rewards and other gifts. More damaging is the use of fraudulent transcripts, altered admissions test scores, and grades granted for phantom courses, and counselling athletes to take courses that will retain their eligibility but will not move them toward graduation (Underwood 1984). One participant in this study referred to this latter practice as "being hooked up," when in fact the students are being exploited for their athletic talents. The real loser is the student athlete, who will lack the education and training he or she needs to survive in the work environment.

The need for big-time collegiate athletes has opened the door for what is called the "slave trade." Independent scouts, for a fee paid by the four-year college, search out talented but academically high-risk athletes and place them in accommodating junior colleges, where their athletic skills are developed further while they earn the grades to transfer to the sponsor four-year school (Edwards 1985).

Below are anecdotal examples of scandals involving Black student athletes in the United States, which has significance to this study because many of the participants cited similar practices on a lesser level:

> In 1984, Chris Washburn, after being recruited by 150 schools to play basketball, enrolled at North Carolina State University. Washburn had a [combined] score of 470 on the Scholastic Aptitude Test, which was only 70 points higher than the lowest possible score, only 10 points higher than a purely random marking of the test, and considerably lower than the average for the university's entering freshmen of 1,030 (Edwards 1985).

> Kevin Ross played three years on a full scholarship at Creighton University, even though he could neither read nor write beyond the second-grade level (Edwards 1985).

A lawsuit was brought by eight black athletes against California State University, Los Angeles, which alleged that: (1) one athlete who scored [a combined] 450 on the SAT was credited with a score of 900 because a surrogate retook the test in his name; (2) one athlete majored in criminology for four years but never took a criminology course, having been counselled to take such courses as badminton, rugby, and backpacking instead; and (3) because of easy courses and surrogate test takers some athletes who could be classified as functionally illiterate were on the Dean's List with 3.5 and higher grade point averages (Ofari 1979).

Commenting on sports in Canada, Kidd states:

Sixty-six percent of the assessment that [the federal government] will use to allocate the next round of cuts to national organizations will be used upon high performance criteria. The jobs, grants, and kudos will still go to the coach and program who win, not the ones who nurture intelligent, mature whole persons (1995: 10).

The pressure to win becomes very problematic for Black male student athletes when it is combined with factors such as poor academic training, lack of nurturing support systems and the overemphasis on sports in the Black community. This focus leads Black student athletes to place less emphasis on intellectual pursuits and devote more attention to sport.

Chapter 4

Systemic Problems Faced by Black Students

If education can destroy ignorance and open doors, miseducation can academically marginalize and close doors. —Dana Brooks

More than two hundred years of British dominance and privilege have put Blacks behind in the race of life and have effectively structured Canadian society around British superiority, values, customs and institutions. Throughout Canada's history, the British elite have exercised their social, economic and political advantages.

Black Africans arrived in this country forcibly uprooted from their own cultures and then had another culture—that of slavery—imposed upon them. Slavery was a state of enforced dependence and inferiority which offered no future. The dominant culture devalued Black cultures and many Blacks, in turn, developed a negative self-image. After the abolition of slavery, widespread discrimination denied Blacks access to education and the political and economic mainstream. As a result, Blacks were at the lowest level in society, nominally free but economically enslaved. These conditions are echoed today by systemic racial discrimination.

Those who educate must begin to share, critically, with students their comprehensive knowledge of all the factors that have shaped and molded Canadian history, politics, social attitudes, economics and culture. However, this is not happening! The problem results in a clash of cultures, a conflict of interests and a struggle for power. There is a contest between proponents of tradition and proponents of change, between those who look to the past and those who look to the future, between old ideas and new ideas, and between historically included groups and historically excluded groups.

The Black community has traditionally viewed education as a path leading away from poverty, inequity and despair. In an historical context, the withholding of education was used as a means of maintaining control over the slave population. It was illegal to teach slaves to read and write. In fact, teaching literacy skills to slaves was punishable by death. This denial of the fundamental right to education created a burning desire among slaves to learn. Yet, while the Black community continues to espouse the importance of getting a good education, Black youth are still not successful in the educational system. High dropout rates, suspensions, expulsions, enrolment in non-academic courses, and placement in lower-track and special education classes are common among Black students.

This situation has left the Black community with no other alternative but to press schools for more input into the schooling of their youth. They are frustrated with the declining educational achievement of their off-spring.

In Ontario, Black parents and educators have become increasingly concerned about the dropout problem and its effects on their communities. They have questioned whether the schools are equipping Black youth with the skills and knowledge essential to their survival in Canada and the global community.

Like everyone else, Black students want to move forward and succeed and, despite the systemic problems they face at scool, many see education as the way to do so. Kirk, an OAC student who aspires to be a professional football player and entrepreneur, stated:

> [Education] is real important to me because, even if I do make it to the CFL, they don't really pay too much. I hear a lot of guys have to work during the off season (June 1, 1994).

Mo agreed:

> [Education] is very important. I want a decent job so I can take care of my family. If I don't make it through ball, I had better have a good education (May 31, 1994).

Fazil, an OAC student, stated:

> I plan to go to university. That is the only way I will be able to realize my dream of being an accountant. I'll probably have to do four to five years of university, but it will be worth it, having a good job and the finer things in life. But nothing just happens. You have to work for it (June 11, 1994).

Damion, a grade twelve student athlete born in Canada, talked about the importance of his academic aspirations:

> I just don't want to end up like so many of the brothers out there. They have so much skill—they got hoops, they got a handle and

they got range—but they ain't got no grades and they end up going nowhere. Every year the same thing happens right here at this school, and it's almost always one of the brothers. I just don't want to end up like that; there are enough of us like that right now (July 5, 1994).

Lou, a grade ten student, agreed:

I just don't want to be one of them niggers that can't speak or write; to me that is damn embarrassing for all of us, because that's what they expect. Well, I'm not down with that (July 29, 1994).

Damion also says:

Hey, I'm not stupid. I see what is around me. I'm Black, my friends and family are Black, and most of them are in some shit job they don't like. I don't want that to happen to me. I know I have to be educated. Nobody is giving me a free ride (July 6, 1994).

Problems Faced by Black Students at School

Black students face many systemic problems at school. Dei has examined Black students' experiences in the Ontario public school system and states:

These students have many worries that have a negative impact on their academic progress. They worry about completing their education and not finding jobs. Some students speak about marginalization of their experiences. They are concerned about the absence of Black/African and other minority teachers. While students admit many teachers and school authorities have good intentions, they nevertheless wonder whether good intentions alone are enough. Some students are having a tough time dealing with authority and power structures that are perceived not to work in students' interest. A fair number of students have talked about having to deal with unflattering teacher expectations. Added to these concerns, some students are struggling to construct their individual self and group cultural identities in a school environment that does not adequately highlight their cultural heritage and histories in both the official and hidden school curriculum. In spite of these concerns, many of the youth are succeeding, and they would like that to be recognized by society (1993a: 47).

Limited Future Opportunities

Informants in my study demonstrated an awareness of the society in which we live. They continually spoke of the limited means of opportunity and success outside the sports and entertainment business. Damion states:

> We do [sport] because I guess we think it's the only way we can get ahead. We've seen it happen before, and it's the only way for us to get ahead. If you do take the academic way, it is very hard because you know the teacher doesn't think you can do it with your brains (July 6, 1994).

Marcus:

> It's all about money and opportunity. Sports can provide that for me. Then I can take care of my friends and family (June 25, 1994).

Marginalization of Black Perspectives, Culture and History

Richard, an OAC student who will be attending a junior college on an athletic scholarship in the fall, says that his heritage and potential role models are not highlighted:

> Richard: To be honest with you, it's the sports that kept me there. Everyone always makes a big deal about the academics, but that to me is easy. You read a book and you tell what happens. Think about it, what does that take? But as an athlete, you have to be tough mentally and athletically. I personally find the sports more challenging. School has always been a little boring to me.

> Interviewer: Boring?

> Richard: Yeah, boring. I don't know what it was like when you went to school, but let me tell you, some of the stuff we have to learn is boring.

> Interviewer: Can you give me an example?

> Richard: Sure . . . I'm not sure that some stuff we're taught is relevant. I'm sure I'd be a lot more interested if there was some more Black stuff to read about. Now that interests me—brothers

like Malcolm X and Martin Luther King. We don't talk about them much, except in February. But I hear a whole lot about Columbus, Mackenzie King and those explorers (June 23, 1994).

Stereotyping by School Administrators and Teachers

Many of my student athlete informants said that school authority figures had encouraged them to participatre in sports from an early age. Richard:

> I still remember my grade four teacher who kept encouraging me—actually he was bugging me—to go out for the track team. They must have seen some talent in me even way back then. It started when we were doing something in gym; from then on he wouldn't let up. Who knows? If it wasn't for him, maybe I wouldn't be running today (June 23, 1994).

Lou:

> I think when one of the coaches saw me in gym, he started asking me out for teams. I wasn't even that good, but he kept on asking (July 29, 1994).

The majority of the teacher and administrator informants in this study felt the school plays a significant role in encouraging or discouraging students in all areas of school life. A few informants wanted to place the onus on the student. Dawn, who has twenty-six years of teaching experience and is now a vice-principal, responded:

> [Schools] can play a big role by encouraging students into various sports. At this school, we have tried to tie academics to athletic success. You must obtain a solid 65 percent average to participate. We would be setting them up for failure if they were encouraged only athletically because very few make it to the pros or receive scholarships. We strive to combine the two. The aim here is to hook them into something to help build self-esteem. If we only got the top academic students to participate in sports, then other students wouldn't get the opportunity to build their self-esteem. Sometimes it is a matter of getting them to do something they are good at. It is just a hook (June 16, 1994).

Frank, an administrator, agreed that the school has an enormous role to play. He also mentioned stereotypes and their serious impact:

> I really believe that stereotypes are deadly to those who don't

conform to the stereotype—the Chinese kid who is not a math whiz, the Black student who is not athletic. A teacher asks a Black kid if he is going out for the basketball team: the kid might be a total klutz. How does he live with that? I also think that teachers are not given adequate training. Teachers with the best of intentions, along with schools, aid and abet the stereotyping of Black kids into sports (June 14, 1994).

Ivan, a track coach and biology teacher of fifteen years, presented a different perspective:

It is all about talent. I don't think schools play a role at all. When you have tryouts for a team, it is picked based on the calibre of the athletes. It has nothing to do with colour. As a coach, I go with the best. The only time I might encourage an athlete is as a means to an end. If the parents can't afford to send their kid to school, and the kid has talent, I push them. Teachers and administrators and/or schools who encourage Black students athletically and not as much academically are misinformed. To go anywhere in sports through scholarships, you have to have the academics. At this school, if a kid expresses an interest in athletics, we check the academics. If the kid is eligible, they'll play; if he's not, they won't. But the kid will always be given the opportunity to pick up the academics. Part of the problem is that high school coaches know nothing about scholarships. For example, to be eligible to compete in O.F.S.A.A. (All Ontario) at a semestered school, you have to pass two courses with a minimum of 50 percent. That, to me, is absolutely ridiculous. The minimum to get a scholarship is 60 percent. All too often these athletes aim for the minimum. We need to raise the standards. If it is important enough to them, they'll do what it takes academically (June 16, 1994).

The role of teachers and administrators is significant in a school. Larry, a vice principal with twenty-three years of experience, stated:

We have a lot of power to influence. I don't think that I've encouraged athletics over academics in my teaching career. I encourage full participation in school life. It's a much more exciting place when you do more than academics, and the individual becomes more rounded. Part of the role of the teachers is to find what individual strengths a student has and help them develop those strengths and overcome their weaknesses. If an individual is deemed to have athletic potential, then I try to encourage it, but never at the expense of academics (June 20, 1994).

Olivia, a teacher with two years of teaching experience, agreed:

Sure we have a lot of influence . . . that is probably why a lot of us got into teaching. We felt we had something to contribute, something to offer. Some teachers may in fact misuse their influence and power, but I believe the majority don't. We have the students' best interest at heart (June 11, 1994).

However, racism is alive in public high schools. Students from Dei's (1993a) study reported racist behaviour and attitudes. Leah, a high school dropout, talked about the presence of racism in the school system and its effect on the student.

Leah: As far as I'm concerned, I think everybody has a bias. Everybody. And racism is so prevalent. If you think about it, it's enough to literally turn your stomach. Racism is a very strong force that exists within the system, and it does too much damage.

Interviewer: You mean in the school?

Leah: I mean we have to understand teachers are people too. And there are a lot of teachers out there who simply just do not like Black people. There are teachers out there who do not like Whites or Orientals. And you'll be surprised, you'll have your hand up for days . . . and you will not be answered. And you could have attained a 98 and simply get a 54 because of your colour . . . or whatever that one's bias may be. You'd be surprised. Oh yeah, all the time, all the time. As far as I'm concerned, I have never been given the credit that I deserve. But I know one day I will get it (Dei 1993a: 12).

Nisha lamented what she saw as racial prejudice by some White teachers:

A lot of [teachers] are [prejudiced], and I mean you figure they're so well educated they won't show it, but it doesn't make a difference no matter how many degrees you have or whatever, it still shows. And I mean the way they treat you, the way they talk to you, it's just different than how they talk to other students, like White students and that (Dei 1993a 13).

Almost all the participants in my study stated that racism existed in the school system and mentioned insensitivity on the part of their teachers towards cultural and racial differences. Mo said:

> As far back as I remember to elementary school, they were encouraging me to join the track team. They do it because some are racist. They don't think we have any intelligence (May 31, 1994).

Jermaine, a student born in the Caribbean, spoke of an experience with a guidance counsellor:

> The advice from the counsellor nearly broke my back. I could not believe it! She said I should be making choices by what my "capabilities" are and that she didn't think I can compete in the advanced. I will be left behind. I wanted to hear something like "You can make it just like all the other students there. But you must be prepared to work hard because all those who succeeded worked hard. And I know you can." When I told my mother, she was furious and she said, "If that's where you want to be, you damn sure you will be there" (Dei 1993a: 11).

Dei also found that several students, particularly those born in the Caribbean, complained about the social stereotyping of the Black male as a violent and criminal troublemaker. Parents also voiced concerns about the labelling and social stereotyping of Black youth, including streaming and what they perceive as the steering of male youth into sports and music (Dei 1993a: 13).

Differential treatment is experienced by Black males and females. Nisha, a gifted female student, spoke about the enormous pressure Black males find themselves exposed to:

> I think Black guys have it worse. I do because they pick on those Black guys. They really, really do. The teachers and all the fights; people come to fight the Black guys and you have to act like you want to fight; even if you don't want to fight, you have to fight. And you're pushed to just do sports. You really see it if a Black guy is smart, they don't admit it, like they don't want to talk about it . . . [so] they just want to just do enough to pass, to be like the rest of their friends, just wear the clothes and that's it. I think again . . . they say okay if you're Black and you're smart, it's usually female . . . not male—it's awful (Dei 1993a: 14).

Dei's (1995) research revealed that Black males are placed under heavier surveillance and are more likely to be targeted for discipline. One of Dei's female participants comments:

> I think Black males have it harder because they're stereotyped, they're all bad. . . . Like they see a couple who are just like messing around, or whatever, and . . . not that there are some people over here who are doing good. . . . It's not fair. I don't know why they just can't treat the person who's doing good, treat him, don't just keep putting him down or whatever, and don't put the people who are doing bad down. Tell them, "You shouldn't be doing this." Talk to them, and not just, "go down to the office." [But] then they suspend them. I mean, that doesn't do anything. You're just doing a favour for them (1995: 50).

The student athlete participants in my study emphasized the importance of respect from their teachers and peers. They perceived their teachers as being interested in them only as athletes, and all voiced a sense of frustration at the lack of respect. Sailes (1984) and Edwards (1973) also found that Black student athletes often perceive themselves as being viewed only as athletes, rather than as individuals who may have other life aspirations.

Teachers and administrators themselves acknowledged that they need to be aware of stereotypes they may bring into the classroom. For instance, Ed stated:

> Traditionally, teachers stereotype Black kids as athletes and recruit them for athletic teams. As a result, Black kids are encouraged more in that domain (August 15, 1994).

Similarly, Wendy pointed out that:

> Schools are mirrors of society, and we live in a racist society. We have racist teachers who have racist beliefs; the school is not immune from this behaviour (June 20, 1994).

Craig concurred:

> [Teachers] are just as guilty as everyone else in encouraging Black kids into sports, something to keep them out of their hair (August 9, 1994).

Mary cited her own experiences as a student:

Well, there is the issue of stereotyping, in that Blacks are expected to achieve athletically. That has happened to me as a student as well. I can remember my guidance counsellor telling me to go to a school that was vocational in nature, because it had a great track team. You do see teachers encouraging Black athletes for what is perceived as their natural talents (July 28, 1994).

Low Academic Expectations from Teachers

Of particular interest for this study is Dei's (1993a) research on teacher expectations. He found this topic generated much emotion and anger among his participants. Mario, a participant in a summer job training program, indicated he might be dropping out of school and described his relationship with a teacher as the most unpleasant experience of his school life:

> Being . . . judged by a particular teacher . . . that was the most [unpleasant experience]. . . . I mean that I wasn't expecting that. I mean, you look up to your teachers. They're supposed to be . . . there for you and they're not supposed to judge you. And I was judged by this particular teacher and it wasn't to say it wasn't done behind my back. It was done in front of my face and I wasn't expecting that, so that was a big letdown to me—it was unpleasant (Dei 1993a: 10).

Similarly, informants in my study faced teachers' low expectations. Keith, who was born in Canada, still lives at home with both parents who immigrated to Canada in the late 1960s. He talked about the constant struggle of Black youth to deal with the low expectations that some teachers have of Black students:

> As a Black student, you are usually trying to prove to all teachers that just because of my skin colour doesn't mean that I can't succeed (January 11, 1993).

Ev spoke of the perception teachers have of Black student athletes at his school:

> I don't think teachers really encourage us academically, but they do athletically. When they see you walking down the hall, they think you're a natural athlete. Take me, for example, I'm not a good basketball player, but every year the coach keeps asking me to come out for the team (May 30, 1994).

Igor, a grade twelve student, stated:

> My coach encourages me to do well academically, but that is just because he wants you to be eligible for the team. That way it brings a lot of attention to the school. You see it all the time. When you're finished, that's it—later. They don't care, they're just using us—so we have to look out for ourselves (July 6, 1994).

Basil, a grade nine student, also mentioned this problem:

> I guess teachers push you to do well by telling you if you don't get a certain grade you can't participate, but that is just so they look good. When it's all over, so are you (June 7, 1994).

O.J., a grade eleven student born in Canada, spoke of the role of class clown that he adopted:

> It was tough. I was at the back of the class chillin'. I was the class clown. I figured what the hell, they don't expect me to do well—at least that was my impression—so I didn't. When I did do well, they were always surprised. Some even thought I cheated (May 31, 1994).

Steve, a grade eleven student, echoed these sentiments:

> I don't think I really achieved the way I was capable of achieving. I don't know, I just wasn't into it. A lot of teachers just turn me off. . . . Sure, they say you can get extra help, but they make you feel so stupid. I just stopped going (July 8, 1994).

Special Problems Faced by Student Athletes

Less Time for Academic Study

Student athletes stated that they put an enormous amount of time into their sport. The average time per week spent practising or playing their sport was nineteen hours. Students spent less time on homework: ten students spent between one and three hours per week, ten others spent four to six hours per week, and the remaining five spent less than an hour. Because of time demands, and the physical energy required, Black student athletes may take a reduced course load and seek non-demanding courses that will help keep them eligible.

Less Time to Develop Personal Relationships

According to Jordan and Denson (1990), insufficient time is available for the student athlete to establish and maintain personal relationships. The student athlete misses many of the social and cultural activities which foster broad interpersonal relationships. Black student athletes find themselves associating only with other student athletes, or living in isolation. This may hinder their ability to develop relationships and interact with females. Dei's (1995) research highlighted the tensions that often exist when female students sense a sense of disrespect from Black male students. One female student states:

> I don't talk too much to [the males] because some of them you do talk to, and it's like you pass and you say, "Hi, Bye," and the next time they see you it's like they want to touch you all over your body. And if you tell them no, it's like, "Oh, you think you're this, you think you're that, you think you're better than people." So I really don't talk too much to them (Dei 1995: 51).

Taken as a whole it appears that race and gender impact heavily on the participants' lives. Psychological, sociological, economic and cultural factors also have an effect. The argument often made is that sport is perceived by Black males as a means to gain status and realize opportunity not available in other more conventional ways, and this appears to hold true in the participants' lives.

Chapter 5

Systemic Causes of Academic Underachievement

Racism

Racism is prevalent in Canadian and American public high schools. The interviews brought to life the experiences of Black youth in a system that is slow to encourage and quick to discourage. Race has limited them through stereotypes and expectations that did not challenge them to excel academically.

Essed (1990) distinguishes three different types of racism: cultural, institutional and individual. All are part of Canadian and American society and of concern to the study's informants. *Cultural racism* involves the image of Blacks portrayed in the cultural media, such as books, periodicals and travel stories, in language itself, as well as through religion, art and festivals. At its core is the contrast made between civilized Whites and savage, undeveloped people of colour. One early manifestation of racism was the association of dark skin colour with the word "black," and thus lower and ugly. Cultural racism is also propagated through channels such as advertising. In many TV commercials, for example, Blacks are portrayed as happy-go-lucky performers rapping and dancing to sell a product. Cultural racism is based on images which reflect a deeply rooted prejudice against people of colour.

Cultural racism takes a variety of forms. We have little control over what this kind of racism can ultimately do to us once it becomes part of our thinking. For this reason, many researchers have argued that education is a two-edged sword, the most powerful social force in the history of mankind: it may be used to empower or enslave, to enlighten or mystify, to clarify or confuse, to ennoble or dehumanize. Education is never neutral. Historically, education has most often been used as a socializing device to secure the rights and privileges of those in control, while limiting the opportunities and life chances of those viewed as inferior or unworthy. Education thus employed becomes a force of domination and oppression. By means of curriculum and instruction that celebrates the achievements and alleged superiority of controlling groups and that omits, belittles or distorts the accomplishments of dominated groups, controlling

85

groups are able to maintain their superior position (Smith 1993).

The institutions of a society are the government agencies, businesses and organizations that are responsible for legislating and maintaining labour policy, political policy, health care, education and commercial services and other social structures. When these institutions function to limit the advancement of certain racial or ethnic groups, granting them fewer rights or limiting their opportunities to make use of these rights, then this is *institutional racism*.

Individual racism occurs when the ideology of White superiority and the rejection of people of colour is assimilated into the opinions and attitudes of individuals. It involves discrimination in private relationships and informal contacts. Ignoring Black colleagues by never inviting them for a drink after work or by excluding them from other types of contact among colleagues is a form of individual racism.

My earliest recollection of discrimination and racism was when I moved to Canada from England and was the only Black kid in my class. Wearing a British uniform and having an accent, I was told I was different every day. I remember going home and my parents reciting the familiar "sticks and stones will break my bones, but names will never hurt me," but I remember being hurt, very hurt. Eventually, a soccer game changed the way others viewed me and how I viewed myself.

I remember being told that I had to be twice as good as my White peers to get anywhere. Looking back, that is a lot of pressure to put on a kid. I experienced, and continue to experience, racism every day, much like my informants and many other people of colour. The pain and frustration of growing up different is something that will always be with me— because racism is endemic in our society. It's in the air people breathe, part of our daily lives. It's inescapable and soul-destroying, so deep, so pervasive, so choking that not a day goes by that its ugliness isn't rammed home one way or another. This experience of racism continues to affect Black students in public high schools.

Socioeconomic Influences on Schooling

In this study, the majority of the participants are from disadvantaged backgrounds, as indicated by their comments, which would place them in "the projects" and "the ghetto." The informants are victims of circumstance and should not be blamed for their low social standing; rather, the inequities present in Canadian society need to be analyzed and dealt with.

Throughout the literature on Black youth, the term "at risk" is frequently used. Slavin and Madden (1989) defined an "at risk" student as one who is in danger of failing to complete his or her education with an adequate level of skills. Identifiable factors are low achievement, retention in a grade, poor attendance, low socioeconomic status and attendance at a school with poor students. High-risk factors are race, class, family background, poor academic preparation and lack of goals. Many of the student athletes in this study meet these criteria of being "at risk," meaning an entire generation of Black males are underachieving and could end up functional illiterates. Experience tells me that many of these students underachieve to make a name for themselves, to have some expression of worth, even if that expression is self-destructive.

All informants are focused in their approach to education, being primarily motivated by a wish to continue their athletic careers and improve their prospects in the labour market. Those who find school work difficult, who cannot see why it should be of interest to them or suspect that it is unlikely to improve their chances of employment are inclined to reject the formal curriculum in favour of more immediate gratifying activities such as sports. It is evident from this study that Black student athletes see their participation in sports and their academic eligibility as a necessary means to advance their athletic careers and enhance future job prospects.

All of the Black student athletes believed a post-secondary education would enhance chances of success in the future. They all cited positive relationships between a college or university education and success. It was apparent from the interviews that the participants were concerned about getting an education and wanted to be respected as students as well as athletes. Many of the participants were motivated to take their studies seriously because of their sport aspirations. As one student athlete explained:

> My coach has really helped me. He has monitored my progress in terms of marks. He has told me that if I want to go South, I have to keep up the marks (June 3, 1994).

Coakley's (1986) study supports the claim that high school athletes have higher academic aspirations than non-athletes. These aspirations were attributed to prestige, increased academic support, encouragement and preferential treatment. Such high aspirations may lead to idealistic expectations about collegiate experience. Also, coaches and others may place emphasis on getting an education and staying eligible as a means to receive a scholarship.

Of great concern is the tendency of many of the informants to view athletic participation as a way out of their circumstances. The adoption of the sport culture, and dreams of becoming a professional athlete, can be detrimental, particularly in light of Edwards' (1989) claim that over 95 percent of high school athletes do not play competitively after leaving school. One informant, who wants to play professional basketball, comments:

> When you come from the projects, sports is all you know. This is
> your way out, so you have to be good. I bet most of the pro ball
> players are from the projects like me and had to work hard to get
> out (May 31, 1994).

One goal of this study was to determine whether sport participation would give Black student athletes a competitive edge in the job market. Would involvement in high school sports increase career aspirations? I asked the participants to respond to the question: "What are your career aspirations?" The majority of the participants proceeded to talk about a career in sports, typically the sport they were presently playing. When the participants were questioned further and asked to exclude sports, it became a difficult task. There were many pauses and silences. Eventually the following information was discovered: seven had aspirations of being businessmen, four wanted to be computer programmer/analysts, three wanted to be teachers, two counsellors, two accountants, two sport trainers, two coaches, one a chef, one a mechanical engineer, and one was not sure. The participants had a variety of reasons for their career choices; however, a central theme in their career aspirations was independence and the opportunity to work by oneself to achieve success. When asked what career he wanted besides sports, one student athlete responded:

> (pause) Well, I guess being a businessman. That way I can do my
> own thing. I don't have to depend on anybody. If I do nothing, I
> don't eat (June 5, 1994).

Another informant agreed:

> Business—running our own business is the way to go—because
> they don't want to hire us anyway (June 14, 1994).

Further probing into the issue revealed concerns about racism. Many of the informants believed they would face racial discrimination in employment and would be seen by potential employers as poorly educated, inexperienced, unreliable and more likely to have a criminal record. These prejudices, combined with other stereotypes and biases against Blacks, in their opinion, make it more difficult for them to secure employment than their White counterparts. Thus, many have expressed interest in a career with independence. One informant, who works at a fast food restaurant, shared his experience:

> Working here has made me realize what my mom said is true. If you want to get anywhere in life as a Black person, you have to be better—not as good, but better. That's the way it is. When I first started here, if anything went missing, guess who they would ask first? Sometimes I wouldn't even be working. What a joke. I've been here for almost two years and they still treat me like shit, like they're doing me some big favour (August 11, 1994).

The experiences informants recounted in interviews provide evidence that racial discrimination continues to permeate contemporary Canadian social conditions and institutional practices.

The Cost of Higher Education and the Attraction of Sports

The majority of the participants expressed concern over not being able to attend college or university because of financial constraints. This is a very real concern, and universities are fast becoming the preserve of the affluent. Rising tuition costs, coupled with the drastic reductions in government funding, are denying access to higher education to children from working-class families.

Duffy (1995) found the average yearly university tuition in Canada is about $2,500, but with the proposals to reduce federal post-secondary education grants, tuition fees are likely to double. Graduating students could face debts of from $20,000 (for those living at home) to $60,000 (for those living away). For U.S. universities, costs are substantially higher. Thus, for economically disadvantaged people, sending their children to university seems practically impossible.

This inequity is part of the larger problem of unequal access to power in Canadian society. Those with power are able to dictate how the system will operate, and the system thus preserves their own privileges and power. As long as power remains in the hands of a few, there appears to be little hope for equality of opportunity or condition in Canadian education.

All of my student athlete informants have aspirations for post-secondary education; however, many referred to the rising cost and their single-parent families. Given these limitations, sport appears to be an avenue with endless possibilities. One student athlete expressed his concern about going to university:

> I'm gonna go, but it has got to be free. That's why I'm working so hard now to attract some attention for myself. If I can get a free education that would be real nice. I don't know how else I'll be

able to afford it, because my mom can't do it by herself (June 3, 1994).

Another student athlete agreed:

> See, in this community, going on to college just don't happen without some help. It's just me and my mom, and she has to take care of the little ones as well. There is just no way we can afford those big dollars, and I know she wants me to go. But if I can get a free ride, that solves a lot of problems. I tell the same thing to my little nephews—find a sport that you like and be the best at it. That's your ticket out of here (August 7, 1994).

The way people view themselves in relation to others—in relation to special abilities, achievements, priorities and physical appearance—is termed "self-concept." The self-concept is made up of bits of information about oneself that are used to organize, categorize, evaluate and explain one's behaviour (Markus et al. 1982). When the only university student whom Black youth know and relate to is an athlete, this is their frame of reference for processing information about self. No matter how much parents, teachers or community leaders may stress study, Black youth are aware that the university and college statistics for non-athletic Black males are not encouraging.

Educators and sociologists can debate the question of whether encouraging young Black males to pursue athletic careers is helpful or not, but the reality is, when these young Black men walk through a Canadian university campus, they see what must appear to be an ocean of mostly White faces and blond hair. When they look out on the athletic training fields and gyms, or watch a game on TV, they see a very high proportion of Blacks. This reality will clearly influence the choice to pursue sports.

Theoretical Explanations for Black Academic Underachievement

Many theories have been put forward to explain youth and sports culture. The "cultural adaptation framework" proposed by Fordham and Ogbu (1986) is useful for this analysis, as it offers explanations for Black students' underachievement. Fordham and Ogbu contend that many inner-city Black male and female youth define academic success as "acting White," implying that academic success is the domain of Whites. Fordham and Ogbu also contend that Whites have traditionally failed to acknowledge that Blacks are capable of achieving academically. They suggest that this pattern may relate to Blacks' perceptions of their own academic abilities, through the "internalization of societal perspectives."

According to Fordham and Ogbu (1986), the high rate of poor academic performance among inner-city Black youth is an adaptation to the limited social and economic opportunities they perceive to be available in adult life. There is a perception among Blacks that education does not "pay off" for them as it does for Whites. This perception leads Fordham and Ogbu to suggest that many Blacks discourage their peers, perhaps unconsciously, from emulating White academia. As a result, Black students do not put forth the necessary effort in school work and consequently do poorly in the educational setting. Fordham and Ogbu also contend that the development of these modes of adaptation is not "deviant" or "pathological" but reflects the social and economic realities of the cultural group. They suggest that low academic performance results from the following factors:

> First, White people provide them with inferior schooling and treat them differently in school; second, by imposing a job ceiling, White people fail to reward them adequately for their educational accomplishments in adult life; and third, Blacks develop coping devices which, in turn, further limit their striving for academic success (1986: 178–206).

The ultimate outcome of this mode of adaptation is the development of a status mobility system (Ogbu 1980), which is defined as "a socially or culturally approved strategy for getting ahead within a given population or a given society" (Fordham and Ogbu 1986: 180). A status mobility system is an implicit "folk theory" for "making it." A key assumption is that "a given status mobility system generates its own ideal personality types, distinguished by those orientations, qualities, and competencies which one needs to get ahead in the particular population" (Fordham and Ogbu 1986: 180).

The status mobility system informs the ways in which members of a given population prepare their children for adulthood. Views on child rearing and formal schooling are influenced by ideal images and the characteristics of successful members of the population. As children grow up and come to understand the status mobility system, they strive to "get ahead" in the culturally prescribed manner. The status mobility system of a group is not divorced from the social and economic realities of its members but, rather, reflects them.

One outcome of a status mobility system is the development of an oppositional cultural frame of reference (Ogbu 1980; Fordham and Ogbu 1986). Thus, Blacks "regard certain forms of behaviour and certain activities or events, symbols, and meaning as not appropriate for them because those behaviours, events, symbols and meanings are characteristic of Whites" (Fordham and Ogbu 1986: 181). Fordham and Ogbu contend that those who cross cultural boundaries face opposition from peers and other members of the Black community. They argue that not all members of the Black community accept this oppositional cultural frame of reference to the same degree: some accept it only marginally and some reject it altogether. In summary, Fordham and Ogbu state:

> It is important to point out that, even though the perceptions and behavioural responses are manifested by students, as peer groups and individuals, the perceptions and interpretations are part of a cultural orientation toward schooling which exists within the minority community and which evolved during many generations when Whites insisted that minorities were incapable of academic success, denied them the opportunity to succeed academically and did not reward adequately when they succeeded (1986: 183).

My study supports the "cultural adaptation framework." Many informants suggested that education does not pay off for them as it does for their White counterparts. This surfaced during conversations on academic experiences and career aspirations. Many informants identified a career in business that would provide opportunities for independence and growth as the preferred channel of social advancement. And, most of the informants have developed a "status mobility system which centres on sport participation (Fordham and Ogbu 1986: 180).

Fordham and Ogbu (1986) identify several important issues. First, if striving to be academically successful is seen by many Black youth as the domain of Whites, and getting an education is viewed by Black youth as "acting White" or "selling out," what then does it mean to "act Black?" Second, and directly relevant to this research, to what extent does "acting Black" mean being athletic, and how do Black behavioural expectations influence the formation of academic and career aspirations? Fordham and Ogbu's (1986) models are useful for an analysis of the motivations of Black student athletes, but they do not provide the necessary framework to critically examine the role of the school systems in fostering Black sports culture.

Much of the earlier research on the educational achievements of Black students has centred on student and family characteristics, such as socioeconomic status, educational attainment of parents and other personal traits. The focus of analysis also needs to shift to school-related factors, such as policies and practices within the school or district, curriculum, content and the roles of teachers and other staff, because these factors can be more easily addressed by school officials.

Results of the Failure
to Provide Culturally Relevant Curricula

The Ontario Ministry of Education states that: "Education must respond to each individual's need to develop a positive sense of self. The development of this sense of self-worth will enhance the individual's desire to understand and examine personal interests, abilities and goals, and to reassess them in keeping with the needs of an everchanging environment." However, culturally relevent curricula are only being marginally implemented in our schools. In many instances, the standard curriculum simply does not present the complete facts of history, literature, art, music, or other aspects of Canada's diverse culture. In particular, through omissions and distortions, Canadians of African descent appear only negligibly in the history of national or global life. Thus the Black child is not affirmed by the information he or she receives at school.

The Effects of Stereotyping and Teacher Expectations

In the course of their educational careers, students are differentiated, examined, graded and assessed, and the results have a direct bearing on their future career and life chances. Given the stereotypical White assessment of Black intellectual ability, the economic and social class background of large segments of the Black population, and the continuing racial discrimination in education in Canada, it can come as no surprise that most Black student athletes reported that their intellects were judged negatively and they were steered into athletics.

This study demonstrates the presence of, and relationship between, intellectual stereotyping and racial stereotyping to provide validation for the assertion that stereotypical and racist attitudes prevail in public high schools. Beliefs and assumptions about intelligence, academic integrity and physical superiority were themes articulated by Black student athletes.

An area of concern for the Black community has been low expectations among teachers of their children. The expectations, positive or negative, that teachers hold for specific children may have an effect on how these children are treated and subsequently achieve. Teacher expectations can be defined as inferences that teachers make about the future behaviour and academic achievement of their students based on what they know about the students now. Researchers have examined two types of teacher expectation effects (Cooper and Good 1983): the "self-fulfilling prophecy effect," in which an original erroneous expectation leads to behaviour that causes the expectation to become true; and the "sustaining expectation effect," in which teachers expect students to sustain previously developed behaviour patterns and fail to see and capitalize on developments in a student's potential.

Self-fulfilling prophecy effects are more powerful than sustaining expectation effects, because they introduce significant change in student behaviour instead of merely minimizing change. Self-fulfilling prophecy effects can be dramatic when they occur, but the more subtle sustaining expectation effects probably occur much more often (Good and Brophy 1987).

In *Pygmalion in the Classroom* (Rosthenal and Jacobson 1968), an experimental group of teachers were told they had intellectually gifted students to teach—although, in fact, their students had been randomly selected. At the end of the study, the students in this group showed significantly higher gains in total IQ than a control group of students for whom their teachers had not held such high academic expectations. Although this innovative study was criticized for major flaws in research design, it did present evidence that teachers' expectations influence their students' subsequent achievements.

Researchers have attempted to identify the factors that influence teacher expectations. There is considerable evidence that race and social class—two powerful influences on a multitude of behaviours—play a major role. Dusek and Joseph (1983), in a meta-analysis of studies looking for biasing factors, confirmed the importance of race and social class as a basis for teacher expectations. Good and Weinstein (1986) found research support for the following: teachers tend to respond more positively to higher-achieving children, to females, to higher socioeconomic-status children, to more attractive children, to conforming children, to those who sit near the front of the classroom and to children who do not belong to minority groups. Additionally, teachers seem to formulate their expectations after only very brief contact with their students.

Teachers play an important role. Ornstein and Levine (1989) indicate that in elementary and secondary school classrooms, teacher variables account for some of the academic failures that minority students experience. Their research suggests that teachers from middle-class, majority cultures tend to communicate less effectively with minority and working-class students. Compounding the problem, these teachers may then compensate for the resulting gap by holding lower expectations of their minority and working-class students. There may even be a subtle, unspoken perception that minority and working-class students are academically inadequate.

Murray and Jackson (1982) present an explanation of academic underachievement for Blacks termed the "conditioned failure model." The authors contend that teachers' expectations about the academic achievements of Black students are often negative because teachers perceive the abilities of Black students through a filter of negative group stereotypes. Murray and Jackson maintain that comparatively lower achievement for

Blacks "may be less a reflection of family background or intellectual abilities, than a result of conditioning or reinforcements Black students receive from their teachers" (1982: 277). They conclude that if teachers regard the abilities of Blacks negatively, it is likely that good performance will generally not be attributed to ability, while poor performance will. Indeed, the high status accorded to athletic achievement in the Black community (Edwards 1969) may reduce the perceived importance of educational achievement.

All studies in which race is included as a variable (Cooper, Baron and Lowel 1975; DeMeis and Turner 1978; Marwit, Marwit and Walker 1978; Marwit 1982; Rubovits and Maehr 1973; Simpson and Erickson 1983) indicate that race is an unfavourable factor in teacher expectations about Black students' academic performance. My study also found race to be a favourable factor in teacher expectations for the athletic performance of Black students in particular sports activities. Informants stated that they were encouraged to participate in sports by teachers and coaches.

Teacher expectations can exert a notable influence on students. Students' self-concepts are affected by the conscious or unconscious communication of teachers' expectations through verbal and non-verbal feedback on the students' performance (Wigfield and Harold 1992). Wigfield and Harold concluded that teachers influence students' beliefs in some domains more than in others, and they speculated that academia and sport are the areas where teacher expectations have the greatest impact.

When Black boys (and girls) enter a sport or physical activity class and comments made by their peers and teachers suggest that Blacks are talented in basketball, a "good at basketball" self-concept is developed and strengthened. If the activity is one stereotyped for Blacks, such as basketball, the teacher may single out Black children for praise, which makes it easier for these children to believe they do have special abilities. Once formed, the positive self-concept for basketball can serve as a guide to behaviour, even if the student's skill level does not match the expectations of the teachers. A positive self-concept for basketball can prompt a student to watch more basketball and benefit from the modelling of basketball skills, play more and become more persistent in the practice of difficult skills. A boy student, observing his own improvement, begins to believe he is talented and recognizes the skills emphasized by the teacher. This further development of a positive basketball self-concept can cause the student to look to the future and see himself as a high school, college or professional basketball player. The improvement in the student's skills leads the teacher to conclude that his or her expectations were accurate, further reinforcing the developing self-concept of the student (Harrison 1995).

The Influence of the Hidden Curriculum

The concept of a "hidden curriculum" refers to all the tacit messages and daily regularities, relations, language forms, values and norms that lurk undetected behind and beyond the content of daily lessons and subject matters (Dodds 1985). Through the hidden curriculum, students tacitly learn and internalize "important" norms and values representing the private interests of the dominant groups in society (Apple 1985). The hidden curriculum thus contributes significantly "to the ideological underpinnings that serve to fundamentally orient individuals toward an unequal society" (Apple 1990: 102). In this sense, the hidden curriculum not only guides school life but has important long-term implications for our roles in society.

Through the hidden curriculum, students not only learn to accept the power structures of society and internalize distinctive forms of social relations, roles and moral precepts, but also "are initiated into the myth that bureaucracies guided by scientific knowledge are efficient and benevolent." The students also acquire "the habit of self-defeating consumption of services and alienating production," "tolerance for instructional dependence" and "recognition of institutional rankings" (Illich 1970: 106).

Many high schools seem to have become more interested in the recognition they gain from sports than in the athletes. The student athletes' physical and emotional welfare thus becomes secondary to their sport performance. Many coaches are eager to accept credit for their athletes' successes but little responsibility for their failures.

The majority of schools attended by the informants have a hidden curriculum that encourages Black student athletes to participate by giving them special attention and recognition. Fazil:

> It's all about winning. If they see you as someone who can help, they'll encourage you, drive you home, lend you money for lunch. Just about anything. When you're Black at this school it means you're an athlete (June 11, 1994).

Gil:

> I'm a pretty shy person, but now people come up to me—even girls. If I want to meet someone at this school, chances are they have already heard about me, which makes it a lot easier (June 1, 1994).

However, the emphasis on sport effectively excludes Black athletes from other areas of social life, since it reinforces the stereotype of athletics as being one of the few skills of which Blacks are capable. But given the enormous odds against making a living in sport, it is unrealistic for Black males to aspire to careers in that field. Pushing them into sport is a disservice to them because it fosters improbable expectations of athletic success.

Overemphasis on Winning and Problems of Time Management

Balancing academic and athletic schedules is a problem for student athletes. Too much time is spent practising and playing their sport, compared to studying. Part of the problem is the overemphasis on winning in high school sports. Informants stressed the importance of winning to make the school look good. This pressure forces student athletes to spend an inordinate amount of time practising and competing. This exploitation is similar to that found in American universities.

A study of the time spent by football players at Brigham Young University on football-related activities (preseason, in season, off-season, and spring practice) found that the average player devoted 2,202 hours per year (or 275 eight-hour days) to being a college football player. It has been estimated that college football players devote sixty hours a week during the season to football, and basketball players about fifty-five hours per week to their sport (Edwards 1985). Because of these severe time demands, and the resulting exhaustion, athletes frequently take a reduced academic course load and enrol in less-demanding courses. The result, then, is that the education of athletes in many schools with "big-time" programs is secondary to sport. As Bear Bryant, the legendary University of Alabama football coach, once said:

> I used to go along with the idea that football players on scholarship were "student athletes," which is what the NCAA calls them. Meaning a student first, an athlete second. We were kidding ourselves, trying to make it more palatable to the academicians. We don't have to say that and we shouldn't. At the level we play, the boy is really an athlete first and a student second (Bryant and Underwood 1974: 325).

Chapter 6

Envisioning Educational Success

This study has sought insights into the problematic nature of sport partici-pation for Black students, the role of the school and decisions in the informants' lives that lead them to sports. Too many Black student ath-letes from this study are preoccupied with their sport participation. Many view this participation as a coping mechanism within a society and school system in which they are not valued and have few alternatives for social mobility. Whether real or perceived, this is the reality the informants live and deal with. This preoccupation with sport becomes problematic when it feeds into the existing stereotypes of Black males as being physically able and academically disabled.

Sport continues to be one of the few areas of school life and society in which Black youth are encouraged, recognized and made to feel they can succeed. School systems have to take some responsibility for Black stu-dent athletes' infatuation with sports. The fact that Black males are en-couraged at all levels to focus on sport is often the result of a racist ideology of Black physical superiority held by teachers and coaches who thrive on wins, and of school systems that would prefer to use sport as a pacifier and social control mechanism rather than deal with the more complex issues of flawed school systems, poor teacher-student communi-cation and relations, and low academic standards.

Given the persistence of racism in society and schools, it is not difficult to understand how sport is perceived to be a springboard for Black male student athletes to find their places at school and in society. Many studies have documented the fact that working-class male youth tend to see sport as a means of coping with school (Cashmore 1982b; James 1990; Solomon 1992).

Sport participation has had significant positive effects on many of the informants, who articulated the desirable character traits they have devel-oped. This evidence supports a developmental theory. But the findings also support a zero sum model. Most student athletes stated that they spent more time practising or playing their sport than with their academ-ics. Coleman's (1961) argument about sport participation relied on his findings that athletic participation was the main determinant of social status of male high school students; he argues that students may prefer to invest time and energy in sport activities and neglect academic work that is not valued by their peers. Rudy, a grade eleven student, spoke of the impact his friends have had on his sport participation:

> Definitely, my boys, they always used to drag me out to the gym to play ball. I think it was just because they needed another player, but that's cool, because I'm hooked on a ball now. If you're not playing ball, you're probably going to be sitting home by yourself because that's usually what everyone is doing (June 9, 1994).

Further, it appears from my study that participation in sports increased higher-educational aspirations and thus raised the student athlete's perceived social status. This effect may also be mediated by the educational encouragement of significant others, which is also apparent from the study. The relatively average academic performance of the Black male student athletes is not necessarily the result of focusing too much on athletics. In fact, athletic achievement may actually have provided them with an educational opportunity that would not have otherwise been present. One of the findings of this study is that the image of the Black university or college athlete is often the only connection between the post-secondary school system and the Black high school student athlete. This connection often affects the sport choice of aspiring athletes.

The Need for Anti-racist Education

From the statements of the participants in my study, it is clear that racism is endemic in our society and present in public high schools. For example, the fact that Black students are encouraged to participate in sports, often at the expense of academics, has racist overtones. An important way for education to address the problem of racism is through anti-racist education, a pedagogy that recognizes the presence of racism, sexism and classism in our society and advocates a shared power structure, critical understanding, and concerted action to address inequity, which now permeates curriculum subject areas and school practices.

Anti-racist education originally developed from critiques by community organizations. It emerges from an understanding that racism exists in society and that the school as an institution of society is influenced by racism. If liberation is to be the eventual goal of education, then education must ensure that a discussion of society as it is presently constructed is carried out at all levels of schooling. All the interlocking mechanisms of society must be opened up to analysis, critique and engagement by students and teachers in a "safe" and honest manner.

Dei (1994) outlines the basic principles of anti-racist education, which are useful in our analysis of how to create successful public schooling for Black students. According to Dei, anti-racist education: recognizes the social effects of race, even though distinctions based on race lack scientific basis; teaches that one cannot understand the full social effects of race without understanding the ways in which all forms of social oppression (based on race, class, gender and sexuality) intersect; critiques White male power and privilege and the rationale for dominance in society; addresses the marginalization of certain voices in society and the delegitimation of the knowledge and experience of subordinate groups in the educational system; examines the role of the educational system in producing and reproducing inequalities in society; acknowleges the material and ideological circumstances which affect students' lives; and questions explanations which blame the family or home environment for school problems (Dei 1994: 2).

Educators must understand the structure of the daily realities of minority groups in society and have the political will to work for social transformation in order to eradicate the inequitable distribution of power and resources. They must understand social differences and critique the significance that society has attached to differences in order to justify unequal treatment (Thomas 1989: 12) Anti-racist education demands a critical examination of explanations and practices which misinform and oppress people (Troyna 1987).

Anti-racist education acknowledges that cultural diversity and racial differences are not inherently problematic. Rather, as Thomas (1987) affirms, it is the significance attached to these differences and the way they are used to justify an unequal treatment of minorities that is the problem. Anti-racist education investigates the ways racism rationalizes and perpetuates injustice and unequal power relations in society (Troyna 1987). It examines the histories and practices that prejudice supports, and reveals the origins of racist ideas and how they have been translated into everyday notions that view the immigrant and the Native person as second class (Thomas 1987: 105). Anti-racist education will move educators beyond the comfortable celebration of others' food and festivals, and lead them to examine the more controversial issues of racism, sexism, classism and the hidden curriculum.

When examining the problem of racism, anti-racist education views culture as dynamic and takes into account social class, gender, age, physical mobility, political affiliations, work, and experiences of discrimination (Thomas 1987). Troyna asserts that, if the aims of anti-racist education are to be realized, issues of race and racism cannot be removed from the political, historical and social processes of society. Thus, theories of oppression and inequality which expose racism must be developed.

The issue of power is central to any understanding of anti-racist education and how exclusion happens. Power is the authority to name, tell and retell the histories and experiences of the dominant group (and subordinate groups), while making other ways of telling and other forms of experience less valid. Anti-racist education places minorities in the forefront of the movement, encourages collective action and cooperation (Thomas 1987), and "conceives strategies for change in explicitly political terms which lead to challenges of existing power relations" (Troyna 1987: 316).

Class privilege must be challenged for anti-racist education to be effective (Mukherjee 1988: 26–27). Because schooling in common practice attempts to indoctrinate students into the dominant ideology of equality and freedom, the issue of class privilege becomes important to any anti-racist work. Although most racial minorities in our schools are members of the working class, it is the ideology of equality rooted in middle-class sensibility—the notion that anyone can make it if they simply are committed and work hard—that underpins current school indoctrination. This ideology is, however, false. Dei suggests that an anti-racist perspective critically evaluates the institutional structures for delivering education and how local communities (e.g., parents, families, community groups) interact with these structures (1995: 12).

Dei questions the role of the educational system in reproducing race-, gender- and class-based inequalities in society. He calls for a more inclusive educational system which is responsive to minority needs.

Anti-racist education must be concerned not just with curriculum issues; it must also address the composition of education ministries, education boards, faculty, support staff and students in our schools. To ensure that all goals of anti-racist education are met, community participation by disempowered groups is essential. These groups must play roles in both the classrooms and the boardrooms. Community access to power is one of the first steps that must be taken for anti-racist work to begin in our schools. Thus anti-racist education finds itself within the broader context of anti-racist relations in society. Community involvement in decision-making and all aspects of schooling is of crucial importance to the disruption of dominant racial stereotypes and practices in all areas of schooling.

In his study of Black youth in Toronto, James found that many youth felt that they could "make it" based upon merit, even though they knew that racism existed and presented barriers to their advancement in Canadian society (1990: 101). They had been indoctrinated into the belief that education, hard work and contacts will lead to success. The same youth saw the reality of racism as only a barrier or hurdle to get over, and they seemed to have no concept of institutional racism.

One of the most important findings from James's study is that Black youth believe education to be of paramount importance to the achievement of their goals and aspirations. That is also the case with my study. This finding, coupled with the attitude that racism is a barrier that individual effort can overcome, shows the lack of anti-racist education in schooling. It also demonstrates the need for education to be an arena of resistance, struggle and renewal.

Anti-racist education affirms that teaching should be student-centred, and that the expression of personal experiences is of prime importance in the promotion of anti-racism (Troyna 1987). Troyna states that anti-racist education calls for collaboration and cooperation in the examination of racism and demands greater recognition of students' rights. Student rights and participation in the movement against racism are crucial. Fine (1989) states that, by not enabling students of all ages, social classes and cultures to confront and discuss racism, the educational system is undermining the resolution of racial inequality. Fullan (1982) implies that to say students do not have opinions and feelings about matters such as racism and change is to say that they are simply objects and not human. If students are to be treated as human beings with valuable opinions and feelings, they must be given a chance to speak and participate in the process of change. Thus, again, a step towards racial equality in the school system must be to allow students to acknowledge and discuss the racism they know to be present (Giroux 1989).

The Need to Raise Teachers' Sensitivity

Any strategy of anti-racist education must address teachers' expectations of students. Some teachers in public high schools continue to have low academic expectations of Black students in general, and of Black student athletes in particular. Through interaction with students, teachers and coaches, students are being encouraged to develop skills that reflect the competence beliefs of others. If, for example, a teacher believes and communicates to a Black child that he is skilled in football, the child may develop a self-image of being good at football, even if his skill is average. The expectations of the teacher can motivate the child to practice more, which can eventually increase the child's skill. The problematic nature of this benefit is that it now appears to be happening predominantly in the gym, rather than the classroom.

The student participants in my study felt that teachers need greater sensitivity towards the uniqueness of Black culture and the factors that underlie the attitudes and perceptions of Black athletes. And teachers need to understand that athletes are people too. Not only do they have concerns outside the sports arena, but they are also students striving for academic success. Black student athletes need educators with empathy, who are interested in them as whole persons.

Encouraging Academic Preparation

As we have seen, teachers have tended to have low academic expectations for Black students, and many Black student athletes focus their efforts on becoming a better athlete, rather than improving their grades. However, many institutions are beginning to recruit student athletes with better academic skills and create an environment that recognizes the minority student athlete as a whole person. Although the majority of literature in this area is from the United States, it is still relevant to this study, as many Canadian student athletes from this study aspire to earn a scholarship to a U.S. university.

In 1989 the National Collegiate Athletic Association (NCAA) passed Proposition 42, which eliminated the "partial qualifier" from Proposition 48. Proposition 48 stated that potential student athletes had to obtain a high school grade-point average (GPA) of 2.0 in a set of twelve core curriculum courses, and at least a 700 combined score on the Scholastic Aptitude Test (SAT), to be eligible to participate in athletics during their first year. Potential student athletes who met only one of the requirements were considered "partial qualifiers" and were ruled ineligible to compete during their first year. However, the partial qualifier was allowed to receive an athletic scholarship. As originally stated, Proposition 42 would not allow partial qualifiers to receive financial assistance in their first year; however, it was revised in 1990 to allow partial qualifiers to receive need-based financial aid. In 1991 the NCAA also passed legislation that would limit to twenty hours a week the amount of time an athlete can participate in activities related to their sport.

In 1992 the NCAA passed legislation that will further raise the initial eligibility requirements in Proposition 42 by implementing a sliding scale for the high school GPA and SAT requirements. Now, a potential student athlete with a 2.0 high school GPA in a set of fifteen core curriculum courses will have to earn a combined score of 900 on his or her SAT in order to be eligible to receive an athletic scholarship. And a potential student athlete with a combined 700 SAT score must have a 2.5 high school GPA to be eligible.

Black student athletes have been affected more than any other group by the present reform movement. Black student athletes score significantly lower than their White counterparts on the SAT and ACT (Center for the Study of Athletics 1989). In a study conducted by the NCAA in 1984, two years before Proposition 48 went into effect, it was reported that 54 percent of Black male athletes and 48 percent of Black female athletes who attended and subsequently graduated from the surveyed institutions would have been disqualified from freshmen eligibility by the standardized test requirement. Meanwhile, only nine percent of the White male and female athletes would have suffered the same fate. Similarly, Walker, Smith, Hoey and Wilhelm (1987) reported that 60 percent of the Black football players at the University of Michigan from 1974–1983 would not have been eligible under Propositions 48 and 42.

The reason for poor academic preparation is assumed to be insufficient student motivation. Thus, by raising the eligibility requirements of student athletes, the NCAA is sending a message to potential student athletes to improve academically. Supporters of the current reform movement also argue that these increases in initial eligibility standards will send a message to the secondary school systems that they must also do a better job of educating high school athletes. Little research has investigated the role of motivation in the academic performance of student athletes. What little evidence that does exist suggests that an overwhelming majority of student athletes value a college education (Center for the Study of Athletics 1988 and 1989) and that, at least for Black student athletes, academic motivation is not a predictor of subsequent academic performance (Sellers 1992).

In reviewing what has been done to support the successful achievement of the educational aspirations of the minority student athlete, it becomes apparent that more attention needs to be given to the poor academic preparation of many Black student athletes, which can be traced partly to the Eurocentric school system, which does not put Black history, culture and experience at the forefront.

In many cases, the Black student athlete has started thinking about a pro career as early as grade six or eight. Hundreds of elementary schools compete in organized athletics. Most intervention strategies begin during the first year of high school, and so they have already missed approximately three years of the student athlete's career and life planning (Sailes 1992). Children need to be reached earlier.

Creating Effective Schools

American Ron Edmonds (1979) created the term "effective school," which means a school in which children from low-income and minority homes are academically successful. Edmonds and other researchers (Rutter 1979; Mortimore et al. 1988) found that children from middle-class homes do better on average than children from working-class and low-income homes; but it is also true that in some schools ("effective schools"), the gap in achievement is much narrower (Edmonds 1979). It was Edmonds who stated:

> We can, whenever we choose, successfully teach all children who are of interest to us. We already know how to do that. Whether we

do it or not depends on how we feel about the fact that we have not already done it (1979: 17).

Virtually nothing has changed for Black youth in the school system. The lack of real progress is shocking, particularly so when one realizes that so many of the issues identified earlier continue to resurface.

The effective school research (Edmonds 1979) identifies several factors that correlate with school success for disadvantaged students:

1. *Vision, mission and focus.* Effective schools are said to be characterized by a clear vision and sense of purpose, and a strong, well articulated focus, widely understood and accepted by staff, students and community. The principal has primary responsibility for clarifying the vision and focus. Some implications: High value is placed on leadership training for principals and vice-principals; teachers recognize that they have a role in the school, beyond the confines of their classroom or department.

2. *High academic expectations.* A prominent role is given to academic expectations, which are communicated by principal and staff to students and parents. Some implications: Significant time is spent on task by teachers and students; dministrators demonstrate knowledge and leadership in curriculum pedagogy.

3. *Collaboration.* One of the clearest aspects of effective schools is collaboration between administrators, teachers, students and parents. Effective schools are headed by principals who are committed to share governance and decision-making, who delegate significant responsibility to teachers and clearly depend upon their staff in the running of the school, and who solicit and depend upon community and parental input and assistance in the development and execution of school policies. Such principals expect collaboration among staff members on curriculum design and program delivery. Some implications: An effective school is managed by staff committees, some of which are joint staff-parent and staff-student committees; parent involvement in home activities are part of the curriculum.

4. *Participation, connectedness, sense of belonging and positive school climate.* Schools that are most effective involve their students in the life of the institution and give them a strong sense of belonging and a very active role to play in the school as a whole. This includes activities which are co-curricular, such as sports, student government and special interest groups, as well as the program and curriculum itself, through active, student-centred learning. Counsellors and teachers work together to create an encouraging environment. In schools where students report a high degree of satisfaction, they describe teachers and administrators as approachable and friendly, willing to listen to a student for a few minutes

outside of class time and able to relate to students on an individual basis. They also describe clear school policies and expectations, impartially applied. Some implications: A broad, varied co-curricular program is offered, involving most staff members and students; peer tutoring programs flourish.

5. *Relevance and integration.* When a school has a clear focus, staff and students can measure the meaningfulness of their activities and involvement against a common standard. Teachers have a clear rationale for their program, and a common meeting ground across disciplines, facilitating integrated program planning. Guidance counsellors assist students in meaningful education planning. Students are better able to understand the goal of their course work and to make sensible choices among alternatives. A clear sense of relevance is a strong motivator for staff and students. Some implications: Teachers develop curriculum packages which are integrated across academic disciplinary lines and related to post-secondary options and interests.

6. *Monitoring, reinforcement and feedback.* Adults and children depend on constant monitoring and feedback, from themselves and others, to indicate how well they are doing at teaching and learning. In effective schools, teachers frequently diagnostically monitor their programs and their students' progress. As a result, they are quickly alerted to both individual problems in understanding, and general problems with the program. They are able to give students feedback when it's needed and to give positive reinforcement to increase motivation. They also solicit feedback from their students on aspects of the curriculum, such as level of difficulty, inherent interest etc. Administrative and staff committees perform the same kind of frequent and rapid monitoring of overall school and program efforts and progress toward stated goals. They recognize and reward successful efforts and discontinue ineffective ones. Some implications: Students are expected to help teachers evaluate and modify curriculum; new program and curriculum proposals are evaluated by cross-disciplinary committees.

Research suggests that a critical factor for success with at-risk students is early intervention efforts. One early intervention program that has had success is the Head Start Program, a preschool program that serves children and their parents. Head Start children have been retained in grade more frequently through high school and placed in special education classes less frequently than their peers who did not attend Head Start (Grimmett and Garrett 1989).

Special Programs for Black Male Students

There has been no ceremony or ritual for Black males like the Jewish bar mitzvah to usher them into proper manhood. Nobody has officially told them when they have attained manhood. This is compounded by the racist oppression of the Black male's capacity to thrive in the marketplace (Hare and Hare 1985). Thus, an array of privileges have been denied to most Black males. For minority males, early intervention and prevention are the keys to practical action plans that can turn the tide of academic failure. Effective programs for Black male students would share common ideals.

1. *Appropriate male models and male bonding.* My experience working with Black youth has led me to the assumption that Black male students suffer from a lack of appropriate male models in their neighbourhoods, at home and in the schools; and that they have few steady Black male contacts with whom to bond. Moreover, these children "are surrounded by an over-abundance of negative images of Black men" (Prince 1990: 3). Thus, effective programs offer positive images of Black male adulthood through Black male teachers, mentors, advocates and other role models, and provide an all-male classroom. Creating all-male classes from kindergarten through third grade, taught by male teachers, would provide young Black boys with consistent, positive and literate Black role models in the classroom. It would also help overcome many of the negative attitudes towards education that researchers suggest hamper Black boys' academic achievements.

2. *Transition to manhood.* Fatherless homes may engender particularly difficult transitions from boyhood to manhood. Many adolescents who are having difficulty moving toward manhood participate in gangs as a form of initiation. Possibly the most innovative aspect of special male programs, therefore, is their use of "initiation rites" to direct and dignify the transition from boyhood to manhood. These initiation programs generally cover a year and often include acquiring new knowledge and rules of conduct, keeping a journal, creating a genealogical chart of the boy's immediate and extended family, providing community service and, finally, participating in a special ceremony (Hare and Hare 1985; Hill 1987). Because public school curricula do not normally include such materials, instructions for initiation rites are often introduced in the form of packaged programs and consultants from the private sector. A further consideration for this kind of program is the suffering of women at the hands of men. Violence against women has an overwhelmingly male cast. Since aggressiveness is a trait often defined as masculine, many men may view this behaviour as the norm. The White Ribbon campaign, started in 1991 by a handful of men in Ontario and Quebec, speaks out against violence against women by encouragng the wearing of a white ribbon

during the lead-up to the anniversary of the massacre of the fourteen women at the University of Montreal engineering school. The white ribbon symbolizes male opposition to violence against women. The campaign also recognizes the need to reach young men to nip the problem in the bud and focuses its efforts in the schools.

3. *Cultural inoculation.* A third major component is the infusion of Black history, an Afrocentric curriculum and African and African-American cultural elements. This strategy goes beyond the usual critique of Eurocentrism and the need for multicultural programming; multicultural programs help to rectify the narrowness of a Eurocentric curriculum and to reduce intergroup conflict by increasing awareness of diversity. By contrast, the aim of an Afrocentric curriculum is less to improve intergroup relations in a multiracial society than to protect Blacks against the hostile forces of prejudice, poverty, drugs, disease and so on. This cultural inoculation has two distinct but interrelated foci: (1) issues of identity and self-esteem and (2) academic skills and values.

4. *Identity and self-esteem.* The self-esteem of Black male students in inner-city neighbourhoods is battered by pervasive negative images of Blacks—on the streets, in the schools and in the media. Because teachers themselves are often affected by such images, causing them to doubt their Black male students' chances for success, the first step is often retraining or even selection of new teachers for these programs. Programs then attempt a kind of consciousness-raising, by teaching the bicontinental history of Africans, making clear the achievements and contributions of Blacks in both Africa and North America to the democratic, scientific and artistic heritage. A related assumption here is that an interesting, relevant and historically accurate curriculum increases motivation and improves performance.

5. *Academic values and social skills.* The values and self-discipline necessary for achievement are thought to be absent in much of ghetto life. Effective programs for young Black, therefore, attempt to combat the "fear of acting White" (Ogbu 1980) that hinders school achievement, and they promote an alternative system of Black values and social skills that will facilitate success at school and in the work world. Culture and history are used to encourage school achievement that does not pose a threat to racial identity. At the same time, the programs create strict attendance rules, give assistance with school work, teach students non-violent conflict resolution and encourage responsible sexual behaviour. Some programs even have uniforms—as simple as standard t-shirts—to create a sense of discipline and camaraderie. The goal is to instill new behaviours that will lead to greater ease with and respect from adults in school and at work.

6. *Parent and community strengthening.* The programs are often di-

rected specifically at Blacks from stressed families. They encourage these boys and youth to become responsible to their homes and community, and at the same time involve parents (generally mothers), guardians, and other community members in the development of these youth. Thus, many programs have a community service component. For example, boys may help elderly people in their neighbourhood. Almost all of these programs try to bring male community members into the classroom as mentors and in other roles, and most demand that parents or other guardians commit themselves to some form of participation.

7. *A safe haven.* Finally, and underlying all other components, is the conviction that many low-income Black males need an environment that shelters them from, and is a positive alternative to, their subcultures. Thus, the programs often protect students from the street by extending the school day and adding Saturday classes.

Programs like these do have critics, who sometimes refer to them as a form of social control. However, my experience as a teacher, counsellor, friend and community worker demonstrates a need and want for such programs from parents, youth and the community, to serve as a shield for Black males from the violence in the community.

Concern has been expressed about these kinds of programs. Some educators worry that they deflect energy from educational improvement and call these programs an abandonment of any hope, faith or determination to force change upon the public education system. Others have argued that programs like these ignore the severe needs of Black girls and may exacerbate tensions between Black men and women. Some say that such programs do not provide opportunities for learning to function in a pluralistic society, and the chance to demystify race through integration is lost.

In 1987, Dade County (Florida) Public Schools instituted one such program, called "At Risk All-Male Classes," in one inner-city elementary school. The program created an all-male first grade class taught by a Black male teacher. Parents volunteered their children for participation. Researchers found that on all academic and behavioural measures assessed, the boys in these two classes outperformed their male peers in a control group that had remained in traditional co-educational classes taught by females. Unfortunately, this program and others have been stopped and complaints have been registered with the Equal Opportunity Commission, arguing that the program discriminates against girls.

My own experience as a teacher of an all-male grade six class was a positive one. We piloted the project out of concern that a number of our male students in general, and Black students specifically, were underachieving. In fact, they were overrepresented in all the indicators of at-risk students. The pilot project provided the students with a male role model, a highly structured, balanced program and high academic expectations. The absence of females in the class seemed to assist the young men in their academic focus and provided the opportunity to group program (talk) about their specific needs. The program only lasted a year, mainly because I was leaving and there was a change in the administration. Nonetheless, it was highly successful, as measured by their standardized test scores, which rose dramatically to an over 80 class average. One of the students went on to be the valedictorian two years later; and in conversations with other students in that class, they believe that year had a significant impact on their personal growth and commitment to learning. Parents and students supported the program, and a similar one was implemented with an all-girls class that was also effective in meeting these girls' academic and social needs.

Chapter 7

What Can We Do?

Summary and Conclusions

Many Black parents still look to the schools as their hope, indeed their only hope, for the future, even though schools have often failed Black children. Typical schools, with their hierarchical and authoritarian structures, do not provide students from diverse cultures with the skills and experiences that will enable them to fulfill their aspirations.

There is startling analogy between this situation and the Vietnam War. The Vietnam War lasted as long as it did because of its racist and classist nature. Neither the decision-makers in government nor anyone they knew had children fighting and dying in Vietnam, so they had no personal incentive to bring the war to a halt. The U.S. government's generous college deferment system allowed the White middle class to avoid the tragic consequences of the war. The people who fought and died in place of the college-deferred were those whose voices were least heard in Washington—the Black, the poor and the disenfranchised. The ongoing problems in Canadian public schools stem from a similar form of inequity. What can we do?

We Can Work Together

The cultural context of the Black community socializes young men to overvalue sports. The solution is not to simply abandon sports, as diminished sports emphasis and participation will not automatically produce more appropriate occupational aspirations and academic preparation. Instead, responsibility for quality education should be placed equally in the hands of schools, students, family and community. Schools need to share power, and the voice of the Black community needs to be heard. Blacks must understand that they are the experts on their own lives and know what their children need. They must be involved every step of the way and equally visible at ball games and parent-teacher conferences.

In the United States, the landmark case of *Brown* v. *The Board of Education of Topeka, Kansas* in 1954 declared segregation in public schools to be unconstitutional. Let us remember the struggle that made that decision possible. The *Brown* decision was the result of Black men and women risking their jobs by signing affidavits which challenged southern White officials. It was their personal courage, determination and strength which finally led to the White-controlled, separate and unequal facilities being done away with.

The consequences of not educating Black youth properly are serious for both the individual and society. Inadequate education often leads to an inability to support a family, higher rates of unemployment, crime, delinquency and higher rates of dependence on some type of general assistance. The cost to Canada is enormous. It makes good economic sense to maximize the use of all potential human resources.

No approach will single-handedly improve the situation for Black youth, but research suggests that educational programming that incorporates early intervention and substantial parental involvement, empowers teachers, and uses community resources and effective instruction can make a significant difference (Kagan 1989; Levin 1989). We would be unrealistic to assume that just one form of schooling will be appropriate for all. Progress has been made—for example, through Toronto District School Board's LEAP (Literacy Enriched Academic Program) etc.—but how much longer should we wait for schools to provide a community of support for Black students all by themselves?

Parents Can Get Involved

Recognizing that teachers and schools alone cannot be expected to raise the aspirations and levels of achievement of their children, parents must also motivate and encourage them to do well in the classroom. Parents must acknowledge and reward their sons' and daughters' academic accomplishments, require them to do homework, emphasize the value of learning and meet and consult with teachers to find out how their children are performing academically. Teachers should take the initiative in welcoming Black parents.

Arthur Ashe (1977) felt a need to warn Blacks about investing themselves too heavily in sports. He urged Black parents to instill a desire for learning in their chidlren, along with aspirations to become athletes. His proposal was for parents to require children to spend two hours in the library for every hour they spend on the playing field, so that if they were unsuccessful in sports, they would have other options. Black student athletes and their families must understand that they are ultimately responsible. They are the ones who will suffer the consequences if the children do not receive a good education. Black student athletes and their families should obtain information about the educational experiences and career status of student athletes from similar backgrounds, and they should critically evaluate the academic support programs offered for student athletes.

We Can Provide Guidance and Enriching Experiences

At present, Black student athletes are rarely being provided with the guidance and experiences that will lead to successful careers. They are not being given opportunities to develop non-sport identities, expand their knowledge of life outside of sport, develop an awareness of the abilities needed to pursue careers outside of sport, establish relationships with people in positions of power, or learn job-related skills.

Career counselling early in a student athletes' academic career has been shown to positively influence the student athlete's career choices and his or her overall academic performance (Nelson 1982). Greater exposure to different career paths increases the chances of student athletes finding a career that matches their aptitudes and aspirations.

We Can Include Black Perspectives in the Curriculum

Like all children, Black childen need to develop a positive sense of themselves. An enhanced sense of self-worth will help them understand and examine their pesonal interests, abilities and goals for the future in a positive light. We should implement culturally relevant curricula in the schools that include a true depiction of Black history, literature, art, music and other aspects of Black culture. Canadians of African descent who have contributed to national life and to the world should be highlighted. Thus the Black child will be confirmed in the value of his or her own identity.

We Can Present Good Role Models

Introducing and providing Black role models whenever possible will introduce Black youth to other career avenues. For example, many Black student athletes attend sports camps during the summer. These camps can provide an opportunity not only to improve the athletic prowess of the participants but also to address their educational, social and personal concerns. During these camps, Black student athletes can be encouraged to discuss educational and career aspirations with Black role models. Far too often at the sports camps, the only role models presented have been university or professional athletes. It is vitally important for Black student athletes to have exposure to role models successful in non-athletic careers, because this experience will provide them with a more realistic picture of career opportunities.

Overglorification of tarnished professional and high school star athletes is another problem—they may be held up as "heros" despite poor academic performance, social misbehaviour or even criminal charges, while professionals and students who excel in other areas are ignored. Our children should be encouraged to emulate the best in all fields.

We Can Encourage True Academic Achievement

Anyone who has ever seen the playbook of a football team will admit that it would take a great deal of intelligence and motivation to master it. In the classroom, scoring 90 percent earns the student a spot on the honour roll; on the football field, the same score earns him only a seat on the bench. A coach will not allow a player to take the field if he knows that player is going to fail once every ten plays. Ironically, some athletes whose academic averages suggest they are functioning below grade level are able to master a playbook that is every bit as complex as a textbook (Sellers 1992). School systems must recognize that Black student athletes have the ability to succeed academically as well as athletically. Nurturing this academic potential will improve these young men's chances at a decent life once their sport careers end.

Today, high school administrators and coaches often ask, or even coerce, teachers to raise the grades of undeserving athletes to maintain their eligibility. The practice is carried through to colleges and universities, where academically ill-prepared Black student athletes are given scholarships. This practice perpetuates the common belief that Black athletes have superior athletic ability, but inferior mental ability.

In theory, athletic participation should be the carrot motivating the student to maintain satisfactory academic performance; if declared academically ineligible, athletes are to be given a warning to get their priorities in order and spend more time studying instead of playing. However, this strategy is inadequate. Systematic solutions are needed. More must be done to motivate and encourage Black student athletes to perform well in the classroom. Negative peer pressure tends to diminish Black males' desires to succeed academically, but this influence can be countered by verbal and material rewards for academic achievement similar to those given for athletic performance. When we publicly recognize Black academic excellence, we enlarge students' self-concept and academic aspirations. This praise sends a message that education is valued in the Black community. Negative peer pressure, specifically the taunt that Black students are "acting White" if they strive to achieve academically, however, remains a major deterrent to many Black students' school performance (Fordham and Ogbu 1986). More must be done by parents, communities, the media and educators to minimize the social pressures Black, academically oriented students face.

Schools Can Provide Academic Support Programs

School systems must adopt regulations that require competent academic support programs for all student athletes. These programs should have the potential to nurture Black student athletes and focus on their long-term development. A program that focuses on the long-term development of

Black student athletes would emphasize future competence both inside and outside the classroom. Unfortunately, now many support programs are forced to focus only on the short-term goal of maintaining athletic eligibility and fail to develop the athletes' academic potentials. This focus leads Black student athletes to pursue a curriculum that may be to their advantage in the short-term but undermines their pursuit of long-term goals.

One program which addresses this problem is a Toronto District school's B.A.S.E. (Balancing Academics, Sport and Education) program, whose long-term focus emphasizes a holistic approach to a student athlete's development. Skills such as writing, notetaking, time management and reading comprehension are taught to participants and former athletes, and successful members of the community are routinely called on to speak to the youth about their experiences. What has made the program successful is the recognition that sports can have a positive effect on one's life. The emphasis, however, is on the whole student and the need to achieve balance in life. The program highlights the fact that there are few professional sport jobs and the duration of a professional athlete's career is limited. The need to transfer the qualities that make athletes successful (e.g., discipline, a positive work ethic, commitment) to the classroom and workplace is constantly reinforced. The program also provides students with an opportunity to work on their skill development (ball handling) when they have completed their study hall. Guest speakers and role models demonstrate balance by tutoring the youngsters both in the classroom and on the court or playing field.

School systems need to exercise the same commitment to the academic development of Black student athletes as is directed toward their athletic development. Most athletic programs now assess student athletes' physical strengths and weaknesses, and design individualized programs to meet individual needs. The same process should be employed to meet student athletes' academic needs.

We Can Implement Anti-racist Education

From the examples I have given and from the statements of the participants in my study, it is clear that racism is present in our society and in our schools. The need for anti-racist education is evident: schools cannot effectively develop positive responses to cultural diversity without confronting the realities of racism. The starting place needs to be the present reality. Who are the learners and what are their needs? What are society's demands? Who are the teachers? What are their backgrounds? What are the general needs of learners, educators and society in today's and tomorrow's world?

When implementing anti-racist education, one begins from a position of questioning power relations as they affect and shape the lives of racial minorities. Lee (1985) calls on teachers to re-evaluate their positions in relation to racial and cultural minorities. She argues that anti-racist education must also include a thorough examination of classist practices. For example, she recommends a teacher checklist to ensure that parents are not left out of their children's education (1985: 20–23). She suggests that teachers must learn to relinquish fixed ideas about control of their classrooms and involve others in the teaching process. Lee points out that not all parents work nine-to-five jobs and that not all can afford time off from work to attend prescheduled meetings (1985: 20–21). Lee's strategies challenge the middle-class attitudes that pervade our schools by acknowledging that it is racial minorities who can least afford time off from work because they more often work multiple jobs and/or varied hours in our capitalist system.

Simply teaching a unit on racism and its effects is not anti-racist education. Nor is the celebration of culture through food, song and dance. Anti-racist education is a critical examination of the structures that produce inequalities and perpetuate White supremacy in society. It is an attempt to dismantle power structures that exclude racial minorities and marginalize them. In fact, anti-racist education is a strategy to energize the democracy of our society.

Ruddle (1986) states that anti-racist education must examine the school systems, school staff recruitment policies and all aspects of the hidden curriculum. Anti-racist educators can identify and address even the most subtle and covert forms of racism in the classroom and should not assume all is well simply because there are no race riots on the playground. Anti-racist education is not solely a pedagogical issue for teachers; students can also participate actively.

The principles of anti-racist education can be effectively fused with sport if Black students, as James (1995) suggests, are afforded the opportunity to develop the leadership skills and networks of support which are needed to assume positions where they can effect systemic changes. Sports may in fact provide such opportunities for Black youth and thus become a critical aspect of their schooling.

Commitment to substantive change is one of the key elements in anti racist education. Those who struggle to implement anti-racist change must be constantly vigilant and learn to ensure that oppression does not simply take on a new face.

When one practices anti-racist teaching methods, one is not just implementing curriculum guidelines; rather, one is articulating and challenging the relationships among power, authority and knowledge. Anti-racist education has as its root liberation. And it is clear to advocates of anti-racist education that the oppressers are as much enslaved by their methods as are the oppressed.

Teachers Can Reject Stereotyping and Recognize the Uniqueness of Each Student

Teachers have a crucial role to play in reversing the overemphasis on sports among Black student athletes. Teachers are susceptible to internalizing and projecting negative stereotypes and myths about Black males. From this study, it appears that it is now not uncommon for educators to treat athletes in general, and Black student athletes in particular, as having less intelligence, more limited academic potential and greater natural athletic ability. The level of academic expectations seems to be much lower for Black students. Many teachers prefer to view their students as a group rather than as a collection of individuals, and they thus ignore cultural and personal differences. Thus, many Black students are now being steered into athletics and away from academics. Rather than treating all students alike, teachers must take a more individualized approach, one that is sensitive to the unique history and culture of the Black student athletes. Teachers must challenge all students intellectually and provide them with immediate, continual and appropriate reinforcement for their academic accomplishments.

Coaches Can Provide More Support and Guidance

Several Black student athletes stated that they frequently discussed their futures and academic development with their coaches. A good way to provide support and assistance to Black student athletes would be to formalize this form of mentoring. Coaches should be expected to work with teachers, counsellors and administrators to provide a solid support system for the Black student athlete.

We Can Hire More Black Teachers (and Coaches)

Schools can also enhance the educational opportunities of Black student athletes by hiring more Black teachers. This measure will in turn produce more Black coaches, who are more likely to understand the unique experiences of a Black student athlete. Lapchick (1991) has noted that some White coaches are now being influenced by their own stereotypical notions about Black athletes.

Black teachers and coaches may be better able to design programs that will enhance Black student athletes' life chances. Black teachers and coaches also provide important role models for both Black and White students.

Recommendations

Given the findings in this study, in order to encourage and support the Black student athlete to achieve success in all areas of life, including athletics, it is recommended that educators and coaches adopt an athlete-centred system that supports athletes in a holistic way. Such a system provides an environment where these athletes can make thoughtful decisions concerning their futures, free from pressures to win at all costs. The keys to an athlete-centred system include respect for the athlete's human, civil, legal and moral rights; health and safety; and the opportunity to pursue an education (Clarke, Smith and Thibault 1994). Educators and coaches can:

- Make a greater commitment to collaboration between sport and education. The two systems should share the holistic goal of encouraging what's in the best interest of each unique student athlete.
- Consult with student athletes, parents and administrators to determine the needs of student athletes and develop programs to meet those needs.
- Begin the process of educational orientation and career awareness at an early stage in the sports activities of the student athlete, preferably in middle school.
- Establish a B.A.S.E. (Balancing Academics, Sport and Education) program in every middle and high school.
- Remove teachers who offer discouragement from positions of influence and retain and support the many good teachers who try to encourage and motivate students.
- Ensure that coaches are qualified through education and experience and adhere to the best interests of the athlete's development as a whole person. The way to achieve this is through an ongoing professional program for coaches that acknowledges the critical role they play.
- Establish a student athletic association, with representatives from the community, staff and students, to hire and fire coaches at the high school level. This association would also be responsible for implementing workshops and seminars on issues of interest to student athletes and coaches.
- Establish athletic academies, such as a Basketball School, which will provide enrolled students with a live-in environment that combines basketball with a full-time academic workload. Such a school would build on the athlete-centred system and allow close monitoring of its students' academic and athletic progress.
- Replace competitive grade-nine athletic programs with strong intra-

mural ones. The respite would provide the student athlete entering high school with an opportunity to adjust to the new social and academic demands.

- Restrict the number of tournaments, games and sporting events a school is allowed to compete in. This will de-emphasize the importance of winning and emphasize the spirit of participation.
- Implement province-wide eligibility requirements for student athletes, stipulating a minimum 65 percent average to compete.
- Rework sporting-event entrance criteria to include a team's academic as well as athletic achievements.
- Establish high expectations for Black youth. Many students from this study feel they are stereotyped by teachers as being unable to learn, or lazy. It should not come as a surprise that students drop out mentally before dropping out physically.
- Teach Black youth how to monitor their own behaviors in certain situations.
- Establish Project Pride programs (which are about saying no to crime, violence, drugs and academic failure) in elementary, middle and high schools to emphasize the need for Black males to assume personal responsibility for their own circumstances, and to challenge them to succeed academically and provide leadership for their families, communities and schools.
- Provide opportunities for Black youth to become involved with institutions, so they can learn to trust others and function in mainstream society. Effective programs like Boys To Men and Project Pride encourage Black youth to volunteer and be active in the formation of their futures.
- Show Black youth how to negotiate the system. They need to know how to act and talk in line with their audience.
- Consult and network with community agencies to provide support to the ex–student athlete.

These recommendations need to be implemented in schools immediately.

Although the focus of this study is on Black male student athletes, there are implications for the female student athlete as well. Support groups for Black female student athletes and coaches are highly recommended, because they too need a network of support to deal with discrimination and harassment. Publicity and promotion for, and commitment to, female programs is also recommended.

Suggestions for Further Research

More empirical study is needed on Black male student athletes. Especially needed are longitudinal studies that address the influence and effectiveness of academic support programs and explore the psychological issues related to athletic participation on the part of Black students.

Although a great deal of research dealing with race and sport has focused on the plight of Black male athletes (Edwards 1986 and 1989), relatively little attention has been devoted to the Black female athlete. Further studies should include a meta-analysis of the literature on Black college athletes, and the inclusion of Black females is essential to research in this area, because they often have even fewer life options because of restrictions imposed by gender.

Institutionalized sports continue to reproduce male domination, as well as patriarchal gender relations and social structures (Bryson 1990), and various forms of sexual harassment, homophobia and abuse are experienced by girls and women in sport (Lenskyj 1986). Questioning how to theorize about women of colour and sport will focus attention on challenging oppressive, racist systems of power and privilege that are legitimized by cultural beliefs and social codes.

Longer-term research is needed before general conclusions regarding the relationship between sport participation and career aspirations and attainment can be made. Research that uses large representative samples of both athletes and non-athletes from various backgrounds and follows subjects throughout high school, university and beyond is needed to increase our understanding of this issue. Further research should also take socioeconomic criteria (e.g., income, parental occupations and education) into account to allow a more comprehensive analysis of the factors affecting the education and career opportunities of Black student athletes.

A Final Word

Today, racism is still present in sport and education. However, if we, as athletes, parents and educators, truly acknowledge that we are part of the problem and need to be part of the solution, then change can occur.

Sport has been overemphasized in the Black community, and too many Black students are putting all their eggs in one basket, says Harvard medical psychiatrist Alvin Poussaint (cited in Simons 1997). The problem is that sport often draws Black kids away from the classroom and toward the playing field. Black star athletes are glaring exceptions to the norm, yet mainstream society witnesses their successes and is able to sleep at night, imagining that the fantasy of equality is a reality. A parade of Black athletes is presented by the mainstream media and is absorbed by both Blacks and Whites. Naturally, why Blacks do so well in sports becomes an issue, usually answered by racist theories that also highlight mental inadequacies. As Hoberman (1997) suggests, "the idea that the black organism is somehow closer to nature is a very powerful idea in Western culture. In fact, one of the consequences of integrated sports is that it is a racial theatre, and inside the theatre, evidence of racial athletic aptitude is translated into a broader kind of racist thinking about differences. One result is that many young black kids buy into the idea that they are built for sports and sports alone."

Regular sports viewers know that play-by-play announcers tend to describe White players as scrappy, hardworking and smart, while Black players are lauded for their raw athletic abilities. As Isiah Thomas once said, "It's like I came dribbling out of my mother's womb."

Hoberman is right on when he points out the racism in depictions of Blacks in sport; for example, he says, the deodorant commercials of Charles Barkley "play cleverly on tacit racist ideas about the black man's refinement" (1997: xviii). Black athletes have been brainwashed and whitewashed. Sports has damaged and robbed our self-worth and dignity and preserved the myth that we are only physical, not mental. We recognize the significance of the historical boxing victories of Jack Johnson and Joe Louis, who served as tangible proof that Black men can compete against Whites and win. But here we are in the twenty-first century and virtually nothing has changed. How else can one explain the rationale behind Ben Johnson agreeing to a footrace with a horse?

In many ways sport has become a pacifier for schools: the more success their programs have with Black athletes leading the way, the less guilty they feel about the lack of Black accomplishment in the classroom.

But the belief that Black kids need to excel in sports to be socially acceptable raises serious questions about our educational system.

When Tiger Woods won the Masters by a record score, one CBS commentator called it not only important in the world of golf but of tremendous social significance. Wait a second here—he played four great rounds of golf! He may yet turn out to be the greatest golfer of all time, but let's put it in perspective. Golf is only a game, a pastime of less significance than freedom, invention, medicine and the like. That is why my heart was warmed by the reception for one of the great heroes of all time, Nelson Mandela, on his visit to the Toronto Skydome, when he was given an ovation usually reserved for sport stars.

So, what we really need to do for today's Black youngsters is remind them that athletic careers are brief and the influence of all but the most accomplished athletes is minimal. We can also use the title "student athlete" more judiciously: reserve it for athletes who are serious students, for those who have done well in the classroom and those who aspire to.

We need to get today's Black youth thinking about laying the groundwork for this next millennium. We need to point out the next mountain to climb or the next planet to walk on. We need to encourage them to be part of something that will forever change the world.

Some view sport in the Black community as character-building and as a bridge to the larger opportunity structure. Through sport, young men learn discipline, teamwork and self-confidence, and these traits can contribute to academic and occupational achievement. Sport also generates an incentive to do well in school and go on to college and, for some, provides needed scholarships.

Others see sport as a misguided priority among Black youth and believe that schools and the Black community push Black males too much to excel in sports. The emphasis on sports can foster aspirations and identities that rest on athletic performance and the perception that education is less important for the future. This creates a tension between academics and athletics, and Blacks find themselves rewarded for their athletic but not academic accomplishments.

The findings of this study do not clearly confirm either position but suggest that the negative effects of sport participation are mediated by the resulting positive self-concept, which can lead to greater educational and career aspirations. However, more complex "social" consequences of sport participation for Black youth must be addressed through anti-racist strategies. Sports, as Lovell (1991) suggests, is "a double-edged sword," as it is often racism that leads Black youth into sport. Carrington argues that teachers use sport as a "convenient sidetrack" and "control mechanism" for Black student athletes, who are viewed stereotypically "as having skills of the body rather than skills of the mind" (1984: 61). For students, sport is a means of coping with a deviating school system, whereby they are able to exercise control over their own schooling experiences, negotiate school authority and achieve academic success (Brathwaite 1989; Carrington 1984; Dei 1994; James 1990; Solomon 1992).

Racism needs to be eradicated from our schools if we are to provide an environment in which all students feel validated and included. Wright (1994) suggests that changes need to be made within the educational system to benefit not only Black students but all Canadians. The solution to the problem of racism against Blacks lies in the construction and application of a combination of anti-racist and progressive Black-consciousness approaches. Black perspectives, cultures and history must be included in the curriculum.

Steele (1992) points out that the underachievement of racial minority youth stems not from limitations in their innate abilities to achieve and succeed in school, but from systematic racial discrimination which erodes their self-esteem, causing them to withdraw from academic pursuits to protect their own sense of self-worth. This alienation allows them to appear unperturbed by their academic failures; it insulates them and confers an illusion of invulnerability but leads inevitably to more failure and more alienation. To break this vicious cycle, Steele suggests that:

> The student must feel valued by the teacher for his or her potential as a person. . . . No tactics of instruction, no matter how ingenious, can succeed without it. The teacher's role is affirming this potential, crediting [students] with their achievements, inspiring them (1992: 68–78).

The recommendations put forth in this book are a step toward an anti-racist education which will address curriculum content, learning environments, communications, community resources, employment practices and individual behaviours, interventions, professional relationships and full partnerships for parents and communities in decision-making. Such an approach will create an educational experience which is fair, honest, encouraging and respectful for all students, including Black male student athletes.

Select Bibliography

Adler, P. 1985. "From Idealism to Pragmatic Detachment: The Academic Performance of College Athletes." *Sociology of Education* 58: 241–50.

Agar, M. 1980. *The Professional Stranger: An Informal Introduction to Ethnography.* New York: Academic Press.

Akbar, N. 1975. Address before the Black Child Development Institute annual meeting. San Francisco.

Anderson, E.L., J. Warfield, S. Picon and D. Gill. 1990. "Race and the Educational Orientation of College Athletes." *Journal of Applied Research in Coaching and Athletics.*

Anderson, W.H., Jr. and B.M. Williams. 1983. "TV and the Black Child: What black children say about the shows they watch." *Journal of Black Psychology* 9(2): 27–42.

Andrews, D.S. 1984. "The G.I. Bill and college football." *Journal of Physical Education, Recreation and Dance* 55: 23–26.

Anshel, M.H. 1990. "Perceptions of Black Intercollegiate Football Players: Implications for the Sport Psychology Consultant." *Sport Psychologist* 4: 235–48.

———— and G.A. Sailes. 1990. "Discrepant Attitudes of Intercollegiate Team Athletes as a Function of Race." *Journal of Sport Behaviour* 13: 68–77.

Apple, M.W. 1990. *Ideology and Curriculum.* Second edition. New York: Routledge.

————. 1985. *Education and Power.* Boston: Ark.

————. 1979. "On analyzing Hegemony." *Journal of Curriculum Theorizing* 1(1): 10–43.

Armbuster, B.B., and T.H. Anderson. 1981. "Research synthesis on studying skills." *Educational Leadership* 39(2): 154–56.

Ashe, A.R., Jr. 1988. *A hard road to glory: A history of African American athletes since 1946.* New York: Warner Books.

————. 1977. "An Open Letter to Black Parents: Send Your Children to the Libraries." *New York Times,* February 6, 1977, Section 5, p. 2.

Baldwin, J.A. 1987. "African psychology and Black personality testing." *Negro Educational Review* 38(2–3): 56–66.

Bandura, A. 1969. *Principles of Behaviour Modification.* New York: Holt, Reinhart and Winston.

Behee, J. 1974. *Hail to the victors! Black Athletes at the University of Michigan.* Ann Arbor: Swink Tuttle.

Berghorn, F.J., N.R. Yetman and W.E. Hanna. 1988. "Racial participation and integration in men's and women's intercollegiate basketball: Continuity and change, 1945–58." *Sociology of Sport Journal* 5: 107–24.

Beyer, B.K. 1984. "Improving Thinking Skills: Defining the Problem." *Phi Delta Kappa* 65(8): 486–90.

Bloom, A. 1987. *The Closing of the American Mind.* New York: Simon and Schuster.

Blum, D. 1993. "'Graduate Rate of Scholarship Athletes Rose After Proposition 48 Was Adopted,' NCAA Reports." *Chronicle of Higher Education,* July 7, A42–44.

Board of Education of Toronto. 1988. *Education of Black Students in Toronto: Final*

Report on the Consultative Committee. Toronto: Board of Education.

Braddock, J.H., II. 1981. "Race, Athletes and Educational Attainment: Dispelling the Myths." *Youth and Society* 12: 335–50.

———. 1980. "Race, Sparks and Social Mobility: A Critical Review." *Sociological Symposium* 2:18–38.

Brand, D., and K.S. Bhaggiyadatta. 1986. *Rivers Have Sources, Trees Have Roots*. Toronto: Cross Cultural Community Centre.

Brathwaite, K. 1989. "The Black Student and the School: A Canadian Dilemma." In S. Chilingur and S. Niang (eds.), *African Continuities/L'Heritage Africain*. Toronto: Terebi.

Brody, S. 1993. "Minority Report." *Sports Illustrated* (2): 46.

Brooks, D.D., and R.C. Althouse, eds. 1993. *Racism in College Athletics: The African American Althlete's Experience*. Morgantown, W.Va.: Fitness Information Technology.

Brown, M. 1976. *Image of a Man*. New York: East Publications.

Bryant, J. 1980. "Two Year Selective Investigation of the Female in Sport as Reported in the Paper Media." *Arena Review* (2): 32–44.

Bryant, P.W., and J. Underwood. 1974. *Bear: The Hard Life and Good Times of Alabama's Coach*. Boston: Little Brown.

Bryson, L. 1990. "Challenges to male hegemony in sport." In G. Messner and D. Sabo (eds.), *Sport, men, and the gender order: Critical feminist perspectives*. Champaign, Ill.: Human Kinetics.

Burgess, R.G. 1990. *In the Field*. London: Unwin Hyman.

Butt, R., D. Raymond, G. McCue and L. Yamagishi. 1992. "Collaborative autobiography and the teacher's voice." In I.F. Goodson (ed.), *Studying teachers' lives*. London: Routledge.

Canada. 1992. *The way ahead: The report of the Federal Task Force on Sport*. Ottawa: Fitness and Amateur Sport.

Carey, J. 1990. "Study: Prep Athletes Misled by Pro Dream." *USA Today*, November 16, 2c.

Carlston, D.E. 1983. "An environmental explanation for race differences in basketball performance." *Journal of Sport and Social Issues* 7: 30–51.

Carrington, B. 1984. "Sports as a Side Track: An Analysis of West Indian Involvement in Extra Curricular Sport." In L. Barton and S. Walker (eds.), *Extra Curricular Sports: Race, Class and Education*. Sydney, Australia: Croom Helm Australia.

Cashmore, E. 1982a. *Black Sportsmen*. Boston: Routledge and Kegan Paul.

———. 1982b. "Black Youth, Sports and Education." *New Community* 10(2): 213–21.

Center for the Study of Athletics. 1989. *The Life Experiences of Black Intercollegiate Athletes at NCAA Division 1 Universities*. Report no. 3. Palo Alto: American Institute for Research.

———. 1988. *Summary Results from the 1987-88 National Study of Intercollegiate Athletes*. Report no. 1. Palo Alto: American Institute for Research.

Cheng, M. 1995. "Black Youth and Schooling in the Canadian Context: A Focus on Ontario." Unpublished paper. OISE, Department of Sociology.

———, M. Yau and S. Ziegler. 1993. *Every Secondary Student Survey, Parts 1,2 and 3*. Toronto: Research Services, Toronto Board of Education.

Clarke, H., D. Smith and D. Thibault. 1994. *Athlete centered system: A discussion paper for the National Planning Framework for Sport*. Ottawa: Federal/Provin-

125

cial/Territorial Sport Policy Steering Committee.

Clarkson, M. 1995. "In praise of single mothers." *Toronto Star*, August 25, F1 and F5.

Coakley, J.J. 1993. "Socialization and Sport." In R.N. Singer, M. Murphy and L.K. Tennant (eds.), *Handbook of Research on Sport Psychology*. New York: Macmillan.

——. 1986. *Sport in Society: Issues and Controversies*. Third edition. St. Louis: Mosby.

Coleman, J.S. 1985. "Sports in School." *Sport and Education* 1: 6–10.

——. 1961. *The Adolescent Society*. Second edition, 1981. New York: Free Press.

Cooper, H.M, R.M. Baron and C.A. Lowel. 1975. "The importance of race and social class information in the formation of expectancies about academic performance." *Journal of Educational Psychology* 67: 312–19.

Cooper, H.M., and T. Good. 1983. "Teachers' beliefs about interaction control and their observed behavior correlates." *Journal of Educational Psychology* 72: 345–54.

Costa, A.L. 1984. "Mediating the metacognitive." *Educational Leadership* 42(3): 57–67.

Cox, L. 1989. *Toronto Star.* Editorial. June 14, A28.

Cummins, J. 1984. "Bilingualism and Special Education: Issues on Assessment and Pedagogy." In S. Shapson (ed.), *Multilingual Matters*. San Diego: College Hill Press.

Curry, T.J., and R.M. Jiobu. 1984. *Sports: A Social Perspective*. Englewood Cliffs, N.J.: Prentice Hall.

Davis, F.J. 1978. *Minority-dominant relations: A sociological analysis*. Arlington Heights, Ill.: Atton.

Davis, L.R. 1990. "The Articulation of Difference: White Preoccupation with the Question of Racially Linked Genetic Differences Among Athletes." *Sociology of Sport Journal* 7(2): 179–87.

Day, J.D., J.G. Borkowski, D.L. Dietmeyer, B.A. Howsepain and K.S. Sanez. 1992. "Possible selves in academic achievement." In L.T. Winegar and J. Valsiner (eds.), *Children's development within the social context*. Hillsdale, N.J.: Erlbaum.

Dei, G.J.S. 1994. "Anti-Racist Education: Working Across Differences." *Orbit* 25(2).

——. 1993a. "Narrative Discourses of Black/African Canadian Parents and the Canadian Public School System." *Canadian Ethnic Studies* 25(3), no. 2: 36–51.

——. 1993b. *The Examination of High School Dropout Rates Among Black Students in Ontario Public Schools—Preliminary Report*. Toronto: Ministry of Education and Training.

DeMeis, D.K., and R.R. Turner. 1978. "Effects of Student's race, physical attractiveness and dialect on teacher's evaluation." *Contemporary Educational Psychology* 3: 77–86.

Deosaran, Ramesh A. 1976. *The 1975 Every Student Survey: Program Placement Related to Selected Countries of Birth and Selected Languages*. Number 140. Toronto: Toronto Board of Education.

Dewey, John. 1963. *Experience and Education*. New York: Macmillan.

Dilthey, W. 1976. *Dilthey: Selected writings*. H.P. Rickman, ed. Cambridge: Cambridge University Press.

Dodds, P. 1985. "Are hunters of the functional curriculum seeking quarks or snarks?" *Journal of Teaching in Physical Education* 4: 91–99.

Douglas, B., and C. Moustakas. 1985. "Heuristic inquiry: The internal search to know."

Journal of Humanistic Psychology 25(3): 39–55.

Duffy, A. 1995. "The Colour of Learning." *Toronto Star*, February 11, B1.

———. 1995. *Toronto Star*, March 15, A9.

Dusek, J., and G. Joseph. 1983. "The Bases of Teacher Expectancies: A Meta-Analysis." *Journal of Educational Psychology* 75(3): 327–46.

Edmonds, R. 1979. "Effective Schools for Urban Poor." *Educational Leadership* 37: 15–27.

Edwards, H. 1992. "What Does the Future Hold for Blacks in Sports?" *Ebony Magazine* 47(10).

———. 1989. "The Black Dumb Jock: An American Sports Tragedy." In D.S. Eitzen (ed.), *Sport in Contemporary Society*. Third edition. New York: St. Martin's Press.

———. 1986. "The Collegiate Arms Race: Origins and Implications of the Rule 48 Controversy." In R.E. Lapchick (ed.), *Fractured Focus: Sport as a Reflection of Society*. Lexington, Mass.: Lexington Books.

———. 1985. "Beyond Symptoms: Unethical Behaviors in American Collegiate Sport and the Problem of the Color Line." *Journal of Sport and Social Issues* 9(2): 3–13.

———. 1984a. "Sports: The Risky Road to a Career." *Christian Science Monitor*, October 12, 25.

———. 1984b. "The Black Dumb Jock: American Sports Tragedy." *College Review Board* 131: 81–113.

———. 1983. "Educating Black Athletes." *Atlantic Monthly* 252(2): 31–38.

———. 1979. "Sport Within the Veil: The Triumphs, Tragedies and Challenges of Afro-American Involvement." *AAPSS Annals* 445: 116–27.

———. 1973. "The Black Athletes: Twentieth-Century Gladiators for White America." *Psychology Today*, November 1973, 43–53.

———. 1971. "The sources of the black athlete's superiority." *Black Scholar*, November, 32–41.

———. 1969. *The revolt of the black athlete*. New York: Free Press.

Eitzen, D.S. 1992. "Sports and Ideological Contradictions; Learning from the cultural framing of Soviet values." *Journal of Sport and Social Issues* 16: 145–49.

———. 1988. "The Educational Experience of Intercollegiate Student Athletes." *Journal of Sport and Social Issues* 2: 15–30.

——— and G.H. Sage. 1989. *Sociology of North American Sport*. Dubuque: Ia.: Brown.

——— and N.R. Yetman. 1977. "Immune from Racism." *Civil Rights Digest* 9: 3–13.

Elkin, F., and G. Handel. 1989. *The Child and Society: The Process of Socialization*. Fifth edition. New York: Random House.

Epstein, R. 1966. "Aggression toward outgroups as a function of authoriarianism and imitation of aggressive models." *Journal of Personality and Social Psychology* 3: 574–79.

Essed, P. 1990. *Everyday Racism Reports from Women of Two Cultures*. Alameda, Ca.: Hunter House.

Evans, J., and B. Davies. 1986. "Sociology of Schooling and Physical Education." In J. Evans (ed.), *Physical Education, Sport and Schooling: Studies in the Sociology of Physical Education*.

Fernandez-Balboa, J.M. 1993. "Sociocultural Characteristics of the Hidden Curriculum in Physical Education." *Quest* 45: 230–54.

Figler, S.K., and G. Whitaker. 1991. *Sport and Play in American Life: A Textbook in* the *Sociology of Sport*. Second edition. Dubuque, Ia.: Wm. C. Brown.

Fine, M. 1989. "Silencing and Nurturing Voices in an Improbable Context; Urban Adolescents in Public School." In A. Giroux and P. McLaren (eds.), *Critical Pedagogy, the State and Cultural Struggle*. New York: State University Press.

———. 1987. "Silencing in Public Schools." *Language Arts* 6(2): 157–74.

Fordham, F., and J.U. Ogbu. 1986. "Black Students' School Success: Coping with the Burden of Acting White." *Urban Review* 18(3): 176–206.

Franklin, J.H., and A.A. Moss, Jr. 1988. *From slavery to freedom: A history of Negro Americans*. Sixth edition. New York: Alfred A. Knopf.

Friere, P. 1978. *Pedagogy of the Oppressed*. New York: Harper and Row.

Frey, J. 1986. "College Athletics: Problems of Functional Analysis." In C.R. Rees and A.W. Miracle (eds.), *Sport and Social Theory*. Champaign, Ill.: Herman Kinetics.

Fullan, M. 1982. *The Meaning of Educational Change*. Toronto: OISE Press/Ontario Institute for Studies in Education.

Garibaldi, A.M. 1992. "The Educational Experiences of Black Males: The Early Years." *Challenge* 2(1).

Gaskell, G, and P. Smith. 1981. "Are Young Blacks Really Alienated?" *New Society* 14: 160–61.

Gaston, J.C. 1986. "The Destruction of the Young Black Male: The Impact of Popular Culture and Organized Sports." *Journal of Black Studies* 16: 369–84.

Gems, G.R. 1988. "Shooting Stars: The Rise and Fall of Black in Professional Football." *Professional Football Research Association Annual Bulletin*, 1–16.

Gil, G. 1992. "The African American Student: At Risk." *College Composition and Communication* 43(2): 225–30.

Ginzberg, E., S. Ginzberg and S. Herma. 1951. *Occupational Choice: An Approach to a General Theory*. New York: Columbia University Press.

Giroux, H.A. 1989. *Schooling for Democracy: Critical Pedagogy in the Modern Age*. London: Routledge.

———. 1988. *Schooling and the Struggle for Public Life: Critical Pedagogy in the Modern Age*. Minneapolis: University of Minnesota Press.

Good, T., and R. Weinstein. 1986. "Teacher Expectations: A Framework for Exploring Classrooms." In K. Zwinwalt (ed.), *Improving Teaching: The 1986 ASCD Yearbook*, 63-85. Alexandria, Va.: Association for Supervision and Curriculum Development.

Goodman, N. 1985. "Socialization: A Sociological Overview." In H.A. Faberman and R.S. Pesinbanayagam (eds.), *Foundations of Interpretive Sociology*. New York: Jai Press.

Gould, D., and M. Weiss. 1981. "The effects of model similarity and model talk on self-efficacy and muscular endurance." *Journal of Sport Psychology* 3: 17–29.

Green, K. 1982. *Government support for minority participation in higher education*. Washington, D.C.: American Association for Higher Education.

Grimmett, S., and A.M. Garrett. 1989. "A Review of Evaluations of Project Head Start." *Journal of Negro Education* 58: 367–71.

Hale-Benson, J.E. 1986. *Black children: Their roots, culture and learning styles*. Baltimore: John Hopkins University Press.

Hammersley, M. 1990. *Classroom Ethnography: Empirical and Methodological Essays*. Toronto: OISE Press.

Hanks, M. 1979. "Race, Sexual Status and Athletes in the Process of Educational

Achievement." *Social Science Quarterly* 60: 482–96.

Hare, N., and J. Hare. 1985. *Bringing the Black Boy to Manhood: The Passage*. San Francisco: Black Think Tank.

Harris, M.J., R. Milich, E.M. Johnston and D.W. Hoover. 1990. "Effects of expectancies on children's social interactions." *Journal of Experimental Social Psychology* 26: 1–12.

Harris, O. 1991. "Athletics and academics: Contrary or complementary activities?" In G. Jarvie (ed.), *Sport, Racism and Ethnicity*. London: Falmer Press.

Harrison, L. 1995. "African Americans and Race as a Self-Schema Affecting Physical Activity Choices." *Quest* 47: 7–18.

Head, W. 1975. *The Black presence in the Canadian mosaic*. Toronto: Ontario Human Rights Commission.

Henderson, G. 1988. "Advising Black Student Athletes." *NACAOA Journal* 6: 3–11.

Hill, D. 1987. *The Freedom Seekers: Blacks in Early Canada*. Agincourt: Book Society of Canada.

Hilliard, A.G., III. 1992. "Why must we pluralize the curriculum?" *Educational Leadership* 19(4): 12–16.

———. 1989. "Teacher and cultural style in a pluralistic society." *NEA Today* 7(6): 65–69.

Hirsch, E.D., Jr. 1987. *Cultural Literacy: What every American needs to know*. Boston: Houghton Mifflin.

Hoberman, John M. 1997. *Darwin's Athletes: How Sport Has Damaged Black America and Preserved the Myth of Race*. Boston: Houghton Mifflin.

Hoch, P. 1972. *Rip Off the Big Game: The Exploitation of Sports by the Power Elite*. New York: Anchor Books.

Holland, A., and T. Andre. 1987. "Participation in Extracurricular Activities in Secondary School: What Is Known, What Needs To Be Known?" *Review of Educational Research* 57: 437–66.

hooks, b. 1988. *Talking Back: Thinking Feminist, Thinking Black*. Toronto: Between the Lines.

———. 1984. *Feminist Theory: From Margin to Center*. Boston: South End Press.

Hoose, P. 1989. *Necessities: Racial Barriers in American Sports*. New York: Random House.

Howell, F.M., A.W. Miracle and C.R. Rees. 1990. "Do High School Athletics Pay? The Effects of Varsity Participation on Socioeconomic Attainments." *Sociology of Sport Journal* 1: 15–25.

Humber, W. 1985. "Sporting Chance." *Horizon Canada* 2(22): 518–23.

Hunkins, F.P. 1987. "Sharing our instructional secrets." *Educational Leadership* 49(3): 65–67.

Ijaz, M. Ahmed. 1984. "Ethnic Attitude Change: A Multi-dimensional Approach." In R.J. Samudo, J.W. Berry and M. Lafferriere (eds.), *Multiculturalism in Canada; Social and Educational Perspectives*. Toronto: Allyn and Bacon.

Illich, I. 1970. *Deschooling society*. New York: Harper and Row.

James, C.E. 1995. "Multiculturalism and Anti-Racist Education in Canada." *Race, Gender and Class* 2(3): 31–48.

———. 1995. *Seeing Ourselves: Exploring Race, Ethnicity and Culture*. Toronto: Thompson Educational Publishing.

———. 1990. *Making It: Black Youth, Racism and Career Aspirations in a Big City*.

Oakville: Mosaic Press.

Jhally, S., and J. Lewis. 1992. *Enlightened Racism: The Cosby Show, Audiences and the Myth of the American Dream.* Boulder, Colo.: Westview Press.

Jiobu, R.M. 1988. "Racial Inequity in a Public Arena: The Case of Professional Baseball." *Social Forces* 67(2): 524–34.

Johnson, W.O. 1991. "The Black Athlete Revisited. More than 44 years have passed since Jackie Robinson Broke the Color Barrier." *Sports Illustrated* (August 5): 44.

Jordan, J.M., and E.L. Denson. 1990. "Student Services for Athletes: A Model for Enhancing the Student Athlete Experience." *Journal of Counselling Development* 69: 95–97.

Kagan, S. 1989. Early Care and Reflecting on Options and Opportunities. *Phi Delta Kappan* (October): 104–6.

Kane, M. 1971. "An American Assessment of Black is Best." *Sports Illustrated* 34(3): 72–83.

Karenga, M. 1980. *Kawaida Theory: An Introductory Outline.* Oakland, Ca.: Kawaida Press.

Kerchoff, A. 1976. *Socialization and Social Class.* Englewood Cliffs, N.J.: Prentice Hall.

Kertes, T. 1991. "The best in college hoops." *Sport Magazine* (January):70.

Kidd, B. 1995. "Confronting Inequality in Sport and Physical Activity." *Avante* 1(1): 3–19.

Kirby, S., and K. McKenna. 1989. *Experience research social change: Methods from the margins.* Toronto: Garamond Press.

Koch, J.U., and C.W. Vanderhill. 1988. "Is There Discrimination in the Black Man's Game?" *Social Science Quarterly* 69: 83–94.

Kunjufu, J. 1985. *Countering the conspiracy to destroy Black boys.* Chicago: African American Images.

Lapchick, R.I., 1991. *Five Minutes to Midnight: Race and Sport in the 1990's.* Lanham, Mo.: Madison Books.

———. 1996. "Bigotry Under the Boards: Exploring the Subtleties of Race and Sport." Unpublished lecture at the Salmon Center for Teaching, March.

———. 1988. "Discovering Fool's Gold on the Golden Horizon: Race and Sport Revisited." *The World and I* 3: 603–11.

Lapchick, R.I., with B. Fay and M. McLean. 1996. *Racial Report Card.* Boston: Center for the Study of Sport in Society.

Leaman, O., and B. Carrington. 1985. "Athleticism and the Reproduction of Gender and Ethnic Marginality." *Leisure Studies* 4(2): 205–17.

Lederman, D. 1992. "Blacks Make Up Large Proportion of Scholarship Athletes, Yet Their Overall Enrolment Lags at Division 1 Colleges." *Chronicle of Higher Education* 3, A34–35.

———. 1990. "Panel Examining Blacks and Sports Discusses Possibility of Boycotting Colleges that Fail to Educate Black Athletes." *Chronicle of Higher Education*, A30–34.

Lee, C. 1982. "An Investigation of the Athletic Career Expectations of High School Student Athletes." *Personal and Guidance Journal* 61: 544–47.

Lee. E. 1985. *Letters to Marcia: A Teacher's Guide to Anti-Racist Education.* Toronto: Cross Cultural Communication Centre.

Lee, O. 1991. Interview by Chris Spence, Vancouver, B.C.

Lenskyj, H. 1988. *Women, Sport and Physical Activity: Research and Bibliography*. Ottawa: Ministry of State, Fitness and Sport.

———. 1986. *Out of Bounds: Women, Sport and Sexuality*. Toronto: Women's Press.

Leonard, E.M. 1985. "The Sports Experience of the Black College Athlete: Exploitation in the Academy." *International Review for the Sociology of Sport* 21(1): 35–47.

Leonard, W.M., II. 1988. *A Sociological Perspective of Sport*. New York: Macmillan.

LeUnes, A.D. and J.R. Nation. 1990. *Sport Psychology: An Introduction*. Chicago: Nelson-Hall.

Levin, H.M. 1989. *Accelerated Schools: A New Strategy for At Risk Students*. Bloomington, Ind.: Consortium on Educational Policy Studies. Number 6, May, 1–6.

Lipsyte, R. 1992. "Blacks on the Court: Why Not on Campus?" *New York Times*, March 27, B12.

Lombardo, B. 1978. "The Harlem Globetrotters and the Perception of the Black Stereotype." *Physical Educator* 35(2): 60–63.

Lovell, T. 1991. "Sport, racism and young women." In G. Jarvie (ed.), *Sport, Racism and Ethnicity*. London: Falmer Press.

Loy, J.E., B.D. McPherson and G.S. Kenyon. 1978. *Sport and Social Systems*. Reading, Mass.: Addison-Wesley.

Mable, M. 1986. "The Black Male: Searching Beyond Stereotypes." In R. Staples (ed.), *The Black Family: Essays and Studies*. Belmont, Calif.: Wadsworth.

Marsh, H.W. 1993. "The Effects of Participation in Sport During the Last Two Years of High School." *Sociology of Sport Journal* 10: 18–43.

———. 1991. "Employment During High School: Character Building or a Subversion of Academic Goals?" *Sociology of Education* 64: 172–89.

Marwit, K.L, S.J. Marwit and E. Walker. 1978. "Effects of student race and physical attractiveness on teacher judgement of transgressions." *Journal of Educational Psychology* 70: 911–15.

Marwit, S.J., 1982. "Student's race, physical attractiveness, and teacher's judgements of transgressions: Follow up and clarification." *Psychological Reports* 50: 242.

McCarthy, C. 1988. "Rethinking Liberal and Radical Perspectives on Racial Inequality in Schooling: Making the Case for Nonsynchrony." *Harvard Educational Review* 58(3): 265–79.

McCullagh, P. 1987. "Model similarity effects on motor performance." *Journal of Sport Psychology* 9: 249–60.

———. 1986. "Model status as a determinant of observational learning and performance." *Journal of Sport Psychology* 8: 319–31.

McElroy, M.A. 1980. "School Sport Socialization: A Test of Differential Effects for Disadvantaged Youth." *Journal of Sport Psychology* 2: 105–23.

McLean, H. 1987. "Linking Person Centred Teaching to Qualitative Research." In D. Bond and V. Griffin, (eds.), *Appreciating Adults Learning: From the Learner's Perspective*. London: Kegan Paul.

McLemore, D.S. 1991. Racial and ethnic relations in America. Third edition. Boston: Allyn and Bacon.

Melnick, M.J., D.F. Sabo and B.E. Van Fossen. 1993. "Effects of Interscholastic Athletic Participation on the Social, Educational, and Career Mobility of Hispanic

Girls and Boys." *International Review for the Sociology of Sport* 27: 57–75.

Melnick, M.J., B.E. Von Fossen and D.F. Sabo. 1992. "Educational Effects of Inter-scholastic Athletic Participation on African American and Hispanic Youth." *Adolescence* 27: 295–308.

———. 1988. "Developmental Effects of Athletic Participation Among High School Girls." *Sociology of Sport Journal* 5: 22–36.

Morgan, H. 1980. "How Schools Fail Black Children." *Social Policy* (January-February): 49–54.

Mortimore, P., P. Sammons, L. Stoll, D. Lewis and R. Ecob. 1988. *School Matters*. Berkeley: University of California Press.

Moynihan, D.P. 1965. *The Negro Family: Case for National Action*. Washington, D.C.: Labour Department, Office and Policy Planning and Research.

Mukherjee, A. 1988. *Toward an Aesthetic of Opposition*. Toronto: Williams-Wallace.

Murray, C., and R.J. Hernstein. 1996. *The Bell Curve: Intelligence and Class Structure in American Life*. New York: Free Press.

Murray, C., and J.S. Jackson. 1982. "The Conditioned Failure Model of Black Educational Underachievement." *Humboldt Journal of Social Relations* 10: 276–300.

Murray, N.R. 1994. "Talking about movement: Experienced knowledge of university dance teachers." Unpublished doctoral dissertation, University of Toronto.

Nation, J.R., and A. LeUnes. 1983. "A Personality Profile of the Black Athlete in College Football." *Journal of Human Behaviour* 20: 3–4.

National Collegiate Athletic Association (NCAA). 1992. *NCAA Research Report*. Overland Park, Kan.: NCAA.

———. 1991. *A Description of College Graduation Rates for 1984 and 1985 Freshmen Student Athletes*. Academic Performance Study Report 91-01. Overland Park, Mo.: NCAA Publications.

———. 1989. *The Status of Minority Participation in Intercollegiate Sports*. Palo Alto, Calif.: American Institute of Research.

———. 1984. *Study of Freshmen Eligibility Standards: Executive Summary*. Reston, Va.: Social Science Division, Advanced Technology, Fac.

National Federation of State High School Associations. n.d. "The Case for High School Activities." Unpublished report.

Norris, A.D. 1984. *The origins of the civil rights movement*. New York: Free Press.

Novogrodsky, B.T.C. 1983. *Combatting Racism in the Workplace*. Toronto: Cross Cultural Communication Centre.

Ofari, E. 1979. "Basketball's Biggest Losers." *The Progressive* 43 (April): 48–49.

Ogbu, J. 1980. *Minority Education and Caste*. New York: Academic Press.

Ornstein, A.C., and D.U. Levine. 1989. "Social Class, Race and School Achievement: Problems and Prospects." *Teacher Education* 40(5): 17–23.

Osborne, J.H., B.F. Jones and M. Stein. 1985. "The case for improving textbooks." *Educational Leadership* 42(7): 9–16.

Parham, T., and J.E. Helms. 1985. "Attitudes of racial identity and self-esteem of black students: An exploratory investigation." *Journal of College Student Personnel* 26(2): 143–47.

Parker, W.M., J. Scott and A. Chambers. 1985. "Creating an atmosphere for college students from ethnic minority groups." *Journal of College Student Personnel* 26(1): 82–84.

Peters, M.F. 1981. "Parenting in Black Families with Young Children: A Historical

Perspective." In H.P. McAdoo (ed.), *Black Families*. Beverley Hills, Calif.: Sage.

Phillips, J.C. 1976. "Toward an explanation of racial variations in top-level sports participation." *International Review of Sport Sociology* 11: 39–53.

Picou, J.S., and S. Hwang. 1982. "Educational Aspirations of Academically Disadvantaged Athletes." *Journal of Sport Behaviour* 5: 59–76.

Picou, J., S. Campbell and R. Campbell, eds. 1975. *Career Behaviour of Special Groups*. Columbus, Ohio: Charles E. Merrill Publishers.

Pine, G., and A.G. Willard. 1983. "Rx for Racism: Imperatives for America's Schools." *Phi Delta Kappa* 71(8): 593–600.

Pinkley, D.S. 1987. *Black Americans*. Englewood Cliffs, N.J.: Prentice Hall.

Pollard, D.S. 1989. "Against the Odds: A Profile of Academic Achievers from the Urban Underclass." *Journal of Negro Education* 58: 297–308.

Pratt, M. 1986. "Doing Fieldwork in Common Places. In I.J. Clifford and G.E. Marcus (eds.), Writing Culture: *The Poetics and Politics of Ethnography*. Berkeley: University of California Press.

Prince, T.J. 1990. "Community Service Projects at Morehouse College Targeted to 'At Risk Youth.'" Unpublished paper.

Purdy, D., D.S. Eitzen and R. Hufnagel. 1982. "Are Athletes Also Students? The Educational Attainment of College Athletes." *Social Problems* 19(4): 439–48.

Rader, B. 1990. *American Sports*. Second edition. Englewood Cliffs, N.J.: Prentice Hall.

———. 1983. *American Sports: From the Age of Folk Games to the Age of Spectators*. Englewood Cliffs, N.J.: Prentice Hall.

Radwanski, G. 1987. *Ontario Study of the Relevance of Education and the Issue of Dropouts*. Toronto: Ministry of Education.

Rees, C.R., F.M. Howell and A.W. Miracle. 1990. "Do High School Sports Build Character? A Quasi-Experiment on a National Sample." *Social Science Journal* 27: 303–15.

Rosenthal, R., and L. Jacobson. 1968. *Pygmalion in the Classroom: Teacher Expectations and Pupils' Intellectual Development*. New York: Holt, Rinehart and Winston.

Royal Commission on Learning. 1994. *For the Love of Learning: Make It Happen*. Volume IV. Toronto: Publications Ontario.

Rubovits, P.C., and M.L. Maehr. 1973. "Pygmalion Black and White." *Journal of Personality and Social Psychology* 25: 210–18.

Ruddle, D. 1986. "Shifting the Emphasis in the Multicultural Debate." *Forum for the Discussion of New Trends in Education* 28(3): 70–72.

Rudman, W.J. 1986. "The Sport Mystique in Black Culture." *Sociology of Sport Journal* 3: 305–19.

Rutter. M., B. Maughan, P. Mortimore and J. Duston. 1979. *Fifteen Thousand Hours*. London: Open Books.

Sabo, D. 1988. "Sport, Patriarchy and Male Identity: New Questions About Men and Sport." *Arena Review* 9(2): 1–30.

Sabo, D.F., M.J. Melnick and B.E. Van Fossen. 1993. "High School Athletic Participation and Post Secondary Educational and Occupational Mobility: A Focus on Race and Gender." *Sociology of Sport Journal* 10: 44–56.

Sage, G.H. 1993. "Sport and Physical Education and the New World Order: Are We Agents of Social Change?" *Quest* 45: 151–64.

———. 1974. "Socialization and Sport." In George H. Sage (ed.), *Sport and American*

Society. Don Mills, Ont.: Addison-Wesley.

Sailes, G.A. 1992. "An Investigation of campus stereotypes: The myth of black athletic superiority and the dumb jock stereotype." *Sociology of Sport Journal* 10(1): 88–97.

———. 1991. "The Myth of Black Sports Supremacy." *Journal of Black Studies* 21(4): 480–87.

———. 1987. "A Socioeconomic Explanation of Black Sports Participation Patterns." *Western Journal of Black Studies* 11(4): 164–67.

———. 1984. "Sport Socialization Comparisons Among Black and White Adult Male Athletes and Non Athletes." Unpublished doctoral dissertation, University of Minnesota.

Schafer, W.E., and M. Armer. 1969. "Athletes are not inferior students." *Transaction*, 6.

Schneider, J., and S. Eitzen. 1986. "Racial Segregation by Professional Football Positions, 1969–1985." *Sociology and Social Research* 70: 259–62.

Schoffield, H. 1995. "Looming university fee hikes spark concern." *Toronto Star*, C1.

Sedlacek, W.E. 1987. "Black students on White campuses: Twenty years of research." *Journal of College Student Personnel* 28(6): 484–95.

——— and J. Adams-Gaston. 1989. *Predicting the Academic success of student athletes using SAT and non-cognitive variables*. Research report 20. Maryland University at College Park: Counselling Center.

Sellers, R.M. 1992. "Racial Differences in the Predicators of Academic Achievement of Division 1 Student Athletes." *Sociology of Sport Journal* 9: 48–59.

———, G.P. Duperminc and A.S. Waddell. 1992. "Life Experiences of Black Student Athletes in Revenue Producing Sports: A Descriptive Empirical Analysis." *Academic Atheletic Journal*. (Fall): 21–38.

Shimbey, A. 1984. "The key to higher order thinking in precise processing." *Educational Leadership* 42(1): 66–70.

Simons, J. 1997. "Improbable Dreams: African Americans are a dominant presence in professional sports. Do Blacks suffer as a result?" *U.S. News and World Report*, March 24.

Simpson, A.W., and M.T. Erikson. 1983. "Teacher's verbal and nonverbal communication patterns as a function of teacher race, student gender and student race." *American Educational Research Journal* 20: 183–98.

Slavin, R.E., and N.A. Madden. 1989. "What works for students at risk: A research synthesis." *Educational Leadership* 46(5): 4–13.

Smith, D. 1993. "Higher Education of Cultural Liberation." *Journal of Negro Education* (2).

Snyder, E.E., and E. Spreitzer. 1990. "High School Athletic Participation as Related to College Attendance Among Black, Hispanic, and White Males." *Youth and Society* 21: 390–98.

———. 1989. *Social Aspects of Sports*. Englewood Cliffs, N.J.: Prentice Hall.

Solomon, P. 1992. *Black Resistance in High School*. New York: State University of New York Press.

Spivey, D. 1985. "Black consciousness and Olympic protest movement, 1964–80." In D. Spivey (ed.), *Sport in America*. Westport, Conn.: Greenwood Press.

——— and T.A. Jones. 1975. "Intercollegiate Athletic Servitude: A Case Study of the Black Student Athlete." *Social Science Quarterly* 55(4): 939–47.

Spradley, J. 1980. *Participant Observation*. New York: Holt, Rinehart and Winston.

Spreitzer, E. 1994. "Does participation in interscholastic athletics affect adult development?: A longitudinal analysis of an 18-24 age cohort." Paper presented at the annual conference of the American Sociological Association.

————— and M. Punch. 1973. "Interscholastic Athletes and Educational Expectation." *Sociology of Education* 46: 171–82.

Sprout, G., ed. 1991. *The Sporting News*.

Staples, R. 1986. *The Black Family: Essays and Studies*. Third edition. Belmont, Calif.: Wadsworth.

Steele, C.M. 1992. "Race and schooling of Black Americans." *Atlantic Monthly* 26(4): 68–78.

Steele, S. 1990. *The Content of Our Character: A new vision of race in America*. New York: Harper Perennial.

Stroman, C.A. 1991. "Television's Role in the Socialization of African American Children and Adolescents." *Journal of Negro Education* 3: 314–24.

—————. 1986. "Television Viewing and Self-Concept Among Black Children." *Journal of Broadcasting and Electronic Media* 30: 87–93.

—————. 1984. "The Socialization Influence of Television on Black Children." *Journal of Black Studies* 15: 79–100.

Sullivan, E. 1984. *A Critical Psychology: Interpretation of the Personal*. New York: Plenum Press.

Taylor, S, and R. Bogdan. 1984. *Introduction to Qualitative Research Methods: The Search for Meaning*. Second edition. New York: John Wiley and Sons.

Thomas, B. 1987. "Anti-racist Education: A Response to Manicom." In J. Young (ed.), *Breaking the Mosaic: Ethnic Identities in Canadian Schooling*. Toronto: Garamond.

—————. 1985. "Principles of Anti-racist Education." *Currents* 3(2): 20–24.

Troyna, B. 1987. "Beyond Multiculturalism: Towards an enactment of anti-racist education in policy, provision and pedagogy." *Oxford Review of Education* 13(3): 307–21.

Underwood, J. 1984. "A Game for America." *Sports Illustrated* 54 (February 23): 66–80.

Van Manen, M. 1990. *Researching lived experience*. London, Ont.: Althouse Press.

—————. 1984. "Action research as theory of the unique: From pedagogic thoughtlessness to pedagogic tactfulness." Paper presented at American Educational Research Association Conference, New Orleans.

Varpalotai, A. 1986. "Sport Gender and the Hidden Curriculum in Leisure: A Case Study of Adolescent Girls." Ph.D. thesis, Department of Education, University of Toronto.

Walker, J. 1985. *Racial Discrimination in Canada: The Black Experience*. Canadian Historical Association.

Walsh, C.E. 1991. *Pedagogy and the struggle for voice: Issues of language, power, and schooling for Puerto Ricans*. New York: Begin and Garvey.

Walter, T., O.E.P. Smith, G. Hoey and R. Wilhelm. 1987. "Predicting the Academic Success of College Athletes." *Research Quarterly for Exercise and Sport* 58(2): 173–279.

Whimbey, A., and J. Lockhead. 1983. *Problem Solving and Comprehension: A Short Course in Analytical Reasoning*. Philadelphia: Franklin Institute Press.

Wigfield, A., and R.D. Harold. 1992. "Teacher beliefs and children's self-perceptions:

A developmental perspective." In D.H. Schunk and J.L. Meece (eds.), *Student Perceptions in the Classroom*. Hillsdale, N.J.: Erlbaum.

Wiggins, D.K. 1991. "Prized Performers But Frequently Overlooked Students: The Involvement of Black Athletes in Intercollegiate Sports on Predominantly White University Campuses, 1890–1972." *Research Quarterly for Exercise and Sport* 62: 164–77.

———. 1989. "Great Speed But Little Stamina: The Historical Debate Over Black Athletic Superiority." *Journal of Sport History* 16(2): 158–85.

———. 1988. "The Future of College Athletics Is At Stake: Black Athletes and Racial Turmoil on Three Predominantly White University Campuses, 1968–1972." *Journal of Sport History* 15: 304–33.

———. 1986a. "From Plantation to Playing Field: Historical Writings on the Black Athlete in American Sport." *Research Quarterly for Exercise and Sport* 57: 101–16.

Williams, S.W. 1992. "Classroom use of African American language: Educational tool or social weapon?" In C.E. Sleeter (ed.), *Empowerment through Multicultural Education*. Albany, N.Y.: State University of New York Press.

Willie, C.V. 1976. "The Black family and social class." In R. Staples (ed.), *The Black Family: Essays and Studies*. Belmont, Calif.: Wadsworth.

Wright, E.N. 1971. *Programme Placement Related to Selected Countries of Birth and Selected Languages*. Number 99. Toronto: Toronto Board of Education.

Wright, H.K. 1994. "Like Flies in the Buttermilk: Afrocentric Students in the Multicultural Classroom." *Orbit* 25(2): 29–32.

Wright, O., and N. Allingham. 1994. "The Policy and Practice of Anti-racist Education." *Orbit* 25(2): 4–6.

Wright, W.J. 1992. "The endangered black male child." *Educational Leadership* 49(4): 14–16.

Young, J.R. 1987. "Prejudice and Discrimination: Can Schools Make a Difference?" In L.L. Stewin and S.J.H. McCann (eds.), *Contemporary Educational Issues: The Canadian Mosaic*. Toronto: Copp Clark and Pitman.